The Lutheran Confessions Series

The Formula of Concord

William G. Moorhead

Study Guide

CONCORDIA PUBLISHING HOUSE • SAINT LOUIS

Edited by Kenneth Wagener and Edward Grube

This publication is available in braille and in large print for the visually impaired. Write to Library for the Blind, 1333 S. Kirkwood Rd., St. Louis, MO 63122-7295; or call 1-800-433-3954.

3558 S. Jefferson Avenue, St. Louis, MO 63118-3968
Manufactured in the United States of America

2 3 4 5 6 7 8 9 10 08 07 06 05 04 03

Contents

Introduction

THE STORY OF THE FORMULA OF CONCORD

Martin Luther died on February 18, 1546. A year later, in the short-lived Smalcald War, Lutheran princes were defeated by Catholic forces. As if Luther's death and a military defeat were not enough for the Lutherans to contend with, they all too quickly fell to squabbling about doctrine. How such contentiousness would be handled and which doctrinal viewpoints would be affirmed would mark the future of the church for decades, if not centuries, to come.

The Formula of Concord, published in 1577, helped the Lutheran church deal with the previous three decades of internal conflicts. So did the publishing, in 1580, of the entire set of Lutheran confessional documents in the Book of Concord. Perhaps the Lutheran church would not have survived the 16th-century doctrinal wars without the Formula of Concord. This study will help us to discover anew how the Formula of Concord helps the church today with theological, doctrinal, and daily-life issues

Martin Chemnitz and J. Andreae were instrumental in bringing about the desired concord. Andreae's "Six Christian Sermons" (1573) served as the spark that finally ignited the fire of reconciliation among the divided Lutherans. What was eventually produced was a document in thesis/antithesis format signed near Magdeburg on May 29, 1577, by six chosen theologians. This document was the so-called Solid Declaration. They also signed a shorter version, known as the Epitome. Both are included in the Book of Concord. The Epitome, written by Andreae, was primarily a layman's version.

By the grace of God, the Lutherans rallied around the document.

USING THIS STUDY GUIDE

Each of the study guides in this series on the Lutheran Confessions has 13 sessions that are divided into four easy-to-use sections.

Focus—Section 1 focuses the participant's attention on the key concept that will be discovered in the session.

Inform—Section 2 explores a portion of the Confessions and provides questions that help the participant study the text.

Connect—Section 3 helps the participant apply the doctrine to daily life.

Vision—Section 4 provides the participant with practical suggestions for taking the theme of the lesson out of the classroom and into the world.

May God bless the study of His truth as we celebrate His grace to us through Jesus, our Lord. By the power of the Holy Spirit, may we focus again on the rich heritage that is ours as the people of God in Christ.

The Formula of Concord: An Introduction

1

FOCUS

Theme: A Confession for Concord

Law/Gospel Focus

Because faithful Christians are sinful human beings, the church struggles daily with false teaching and unbelief. God's Word is our truth and standard, but we often fail to listen to and believe the Holy Scriptures. Yet we rejoice in the promise of the Savior, who forgives us and sends the Holy Spirit to lead us into all truth.

Objectives

By the power of the Holy Spirit working through God's Word, we will

1. understand the historical context of the Formula of Concord;
2. appreciate the confessors' reliance on God's Word as the rule and norm of what we believe, teach, and confess;
3. demonstrate a desire to grow in the grace and knowledge of God's Word and the Gospel of forgiveness, life, and salvation in Christ.

Opening Worship

Read together these words from 1 Corinthians 1 as a responsive prayer.

Leader: Grace and peace to you from God our Father and the Lord Jesus Christ.
Participants: I always thank God for you because of His grace given you in Christ Jesus.
Leader: For in Him you have been enriched in every way—in all your speaking and in all your knowledge—because our testimony about Christ was confirmed in you.
Participants: Therefore you do not lack any spiritual gift as you eagerly wait for our Lord Jesus Christ to be revealed.
Leader: He will keep you strong to the end, so that you will be blameless on the day of our Lord Jesus Christ.
Participants: God, who has called you into fellowship with His Son Jesus Christ our Lord, is faithful.

Introduction

After Luther's death (1546) and the Smalcald War (1547), the Lutherans in the Holy Roman Empire were in a precarious position. Without their leader, the pastors and churches faced opposition from the outside and dissension within.

Although the Lutherans achieved appropriate legal status in the Holy Roman Empire through the agreement known as the Peace of Augsburg in 1555 (they could confess and practice their faith freely), they soon were divided over significant doctrinal issues. It was clear that concord was necessary if the *Evangelical* church was to survive.

What was the source and standard of their teaching? On what confessions of faith would Lutheran pastors and congregations stand? The Introduction to the Formula of Concord answers these fundamental questions.

1. Why is church leadership important?

2. Besides the Bible, what are some "authorities" to which people look for their beliefs? How do people generally view the Bible?

3. Why is doctrinal agreement necessary for an evangelical church?

INFORM

The Formula of Concord: Epitome

1. We believe, teach, and confess that the prophetic and apostolic writings of the Old and New Testaments are the only rule and norm according to which all doctrines and teachers alike must be appraised and judged, as it is written in Psalm 119:105, "Thy word is a lamp to my feet and a light to my path." And St. Paul says in Galatians 1:8, "Even if an angel from heaven should preach to you a gospel contrary to that which we preached to you, let him be accursed."

Other writings of ancient and modern teachers, whatever their names, should not be put on a par with Holy Scripture. Every single one of them should be subordinated to the Scriptures and should be received in no other way and no further than as witnesses to the fashion in which the doctrine of the prophets and apostles was preserved in post-apostolic times.

2. Immediately after the time of the apostles—in fact, already during their lifetime—false teachers and heretics invaded the church. Against these the ancient church formulated symbols (that is, brief and explicit confessions) which were accepted as the unanimous, catholic, Christian faith and confessions of the orthodox and true church, namely, the Apostles' Creed, the Nicene Creed, and the Athanasian Creed. We pledge ourselves to these, and we hereby reject all heresies and teachings which have been introduced into the church of God contrary to them.

3. With reference to the schism in matters of faith which has occurred in our times, we regard, as the unanimous consensus and exposition of our Christian faith, particularly against the false worship, idolatry, and superstition of the papacy and against other sects, and as the symbol of our time, the first and unaltered Augsburg Confession, which was delivered to Emperor Charles V at Augsburg during the great Diet in the year 1530,

together with the Apology thereof and the Articles drafted at Smalcald in the year 1537, which the leading theologians approved by their subscription at that time [that is, the Smalcald Articles and the Treatise on the Power and Primacy of the Pope].

Since these matters also concern the laity and the salvation of their souls, we subscribe Dr. Luther's Small and Large Catechisms as both of them are contained in his printed works. They are "the layman's Bible" and contain everything which Holy Scripture discusses at greater length and which a Christian must know for his salvation.

All doctrines should conform to the standards set forth above. Whatever is contrary to them should be rejected and condemned as opposed to the unanimous declaration of our faith.

In this way the distinction between the Holy Scripture of the Old and New Testaments and all other writings is maintained, and Holy Scripture remains the only judge, rule, and norm according to which as the only touchstone all doctrines should and must be understood and judged as good or evil, right or wrong.

Other symbols and other writings are not judged like Holy Scripture, but merely witnesses and expositions of the faith, setting forth how at various times the Holy Scriptures were understood by contemporaries in the church of God with reference to controverted articles, and how contrary teachings were rejected and condemned.

Discussing the Text

1. What does the introduction to the Epitome confess about the Holy Scriptures? In what ways is the Bible unique?

2. How do the confessors regard other writings? Why is the distinction critical for the church?

3. Summarize, in your own words, the faith of the three "ecumenical" creeds.

4. How do the confessors link their teaching with the universal church?

5. How did Luther's catechisms help God's people to know and understand the Christian faith?

6. Why is it important for "average" church members to know Luther's catechisms?

7. What criteria do people sometimes use when deciding which church to join? How can Luther's catechisms help to make a God-pleasing choice?

8. Why do we need doctrinal statements when we already have the Bible?

CONNECT

The Spirit of truth works through the Word of truth—Holy Scripture. In His mercy, God promises to use His Word to save fallen, sinful human beings. He gives His Law to confront us with our need and His Gospel to bring us eternal salvation.

The Formula of Concord: Solid Declaration

> The primary requirement for basic and permanent concord within the church is a summary formula and pattern, unanimously approved, in which the summarized doctrine commonly confessed by the churches of the pure Christian religion is drawn together out of the Word of God. For this same purpose the ancient church always had its dependable symbols. It based

these not on mere private writings, but on such books as had been written, approved, and accepted in the name of those churches which confessed the same doctrine and religion. In the same way we have from our hearts and with our mouths declared in mutual agreement that we shall neither prepare nor accept a different or a new confession of our faith. Rather, we pledge ourselves again to those public and well-known symbols or common confessions which have at all times and in all places been accepted in all the churches of the Augsburg Confession. ...

1. We pledge ourselves to the prophetic and apostolic writings of the Old and New Testaments as the pure and clear fountain of Israel, which is the only true norm according to which all teachers and teachings are to be judged and evaluated.

2. Since in ancient times the true Christian doctrine as it was correctly and soundly understood was drawn together out of God's Word in brief articles or chapters against the aberrations of heretics, we further pledge allegiance to the three general Creeds, the Apostles', the Nicene, and the Athanasian, as the glorious confessions of the faith—succinct, Christian, and based upon the Word of God—in which all those heresies which at that time had arisen within the Christian church are clearly and solidly refuted.

3. By a special grace our merciful God has in these last days brought to light the truth of His Word ... through the faithful ministry of that illustrious man of God, Dr. Luther. This doctrine, drawn from and conformed to the Word of God, is summarized in the articles and chapters of the Augsburg Confession. ...

The reason why we have embodied the writings above listed—the Augsburg Confession, the Apology, the Smalcald Articles, and Luther's Large and Small Catechisms—in the cited summary of our Christian doctrine is that they have always and everywhere been accepted as the common and universally accepted belief of our churches, that the chief and most illustrious theologians of that time subscribed them, and that all Evangelical churches and schools received them. We have included these confessions also because all were prepared and published before the dissensions arose among the theologians of the Augsburg Confession. They are therefore regarded as impartial, none of the parties in the various controversies can or should reject them, nor can anyone who sincerely adheres to the Augsburg Confession object to these documents but will gladly admit and accept them as witnesses to the truth. No one can blame us if we derive our expositions and decisions in the controverted articles from these writings, for just as we base our position on the Word of God as the eternal truth, so we introduce and cite these writings as a witness to the truth and as exhibiting the unanimous and correct understanding of our predecessors who remained steadfastly in the pure doctrine. (Rule and Norm, sections 1–13)

1. In what ways have confessions of faith helped you to understand and appreciate the Gospel?

2. Share how the Scriptures are the "pure and clear fountain" of living water in your life.

3. How does God use His faithful people to witness to His truth today?

4. In what ways can you grow in grace and the knowledge of God's Word?

VISION

Personal Reflection

1. What spiritual concerns might you have if the church fathers had not placed scriptural beliefs in the Confessions?
2. If you were to join another church denomination, what three questions would you ask about their doctrines before you joined?

3. After reading the selections in this study, one might want to leave such "deep" doctrine to the pastors. What risks does this attitude pose?

Family Connection

1. Parents are God's "appraisers" of family life (see the Fourth Commandment and its explanation). Suggest ways that parents can do this most effectively. Which ways seem particularly promising to you?
2. Creeds are statements of belief. Create a family creed that states your religious beliefs. Compare it to the Apostles' Creed.
3. Change your family creed (see previous question) into a short slogan or motto that describes your family's faith. How are slogans or mottos useful?

Closing Worship

Sing or read together "Preserve Your Word, O Savior" (*LW* 337).

Preserve Your Word, O Savior,
To us this latter day,
And let Your kingdom flourish;
Enlarge Your church, we pray.
Oh, keep our faith from failing;
Keep hope's bright star aglow.
Let nothing from truth turn us
While living here below.

Preserve, O Lord, Your Zion,
Bought dearly with Your blood;
Protect what You have chosen
Against the hellish flood.
Be always our defender
When dangers gather round;
When all the earth is crumbling,
Safe may Your church be found.

Preserve Your Word and preaching,
The truth that makes us whole,
The mirror of Your glory,
The pow'r that saves the soul.
Oh, may this living water,
This dew of heav'nly grace,
Sustain us while here living
Until we see Your face.

For Next Week

Read Article 1 of the Formula of Concord (Epitome).

Article 1

FOCUS

Theme: Original Sin

Law/Gospel Focus

All people are sinful from birth. Although we rebel against God and His Word, we are still His good creation. In love the heavenly Father sent His Son to be the world's Redeemer. Through Christ we are rescued from sin, death, and Satan and are destined for eternal glory.

Objectives

By the power of the Holy Spirit working through God's Word, we will

1. admit and confess before God our true sinful condition;
2. rejoice in the power of Christ's death on the cross to defeat the power of sin, death, and the devil;
3. seek the power of the Spirit to struggle against sin and live as light in our dark world.

Opening Worship

Read together these words from 1 Corinthians 1 as a responsive prayer.

Leader: For the message of the cross is foolishness to those who are perishing, but to us who are being saved it is the power of God.

Participants: For it is written: "I will destroy the wisdom of the wise; the intelligence of the intelligent I will frustrate."

Leader: Where is the wise man? Where is the scholar? Where is the philosopher of this age? Has not God made foolish the wisdom of the world?

Participants: For since in the wisdom of God the world through its wisdom did not know Him, God was pleased through the foolishness of what was preached to save those who believe.

Leader: Jews demand miraculous signs and Greeks look for wisdom,

Participants: But we preach Christ crucified: a stumbling block to Jews and foolishness to Gentiles,

Leader: But to those whom God has called, both Jews and Greeks, Christ the power of God and the wisdom of God.

Participants: For the foolishness of God is wiser than man's wisdom, and the weakness of God is stronger than man's strength.

Introduction

In 1560, Matthias Flacius wanted to stress the sinfulness and utter depravity of human nature so strongly that he argued that original sin is "the very substance of man." Although his friends believed he had overstated his case, Flacius persisted. He apparently could not see how his position implicated God the Creator as being responsible for human sin. He also failed to recognize that his position compromised the scriptural witness that Jesus Christ was truly human and without sin. Article 1 of the Formula of Concord addresses this key issue for God's people.

1. What comes to mind when you think of sin?

2. Why is it difficult for people to accept the truth of *original* sin?

INFORM

The Formula of Concord: Epitome

The principal question in this controversy is if, strictly and without any distinction, original sin is man's corrupted nature, substance, and essence, or indeed the principal and best part of his being (that is, his rational soul in its highest form and powers). Or if there is a distinction, even after the Fall, between man's substance, nature, essence, body, and soul on the one hand, and original sin on the other hand, so that man's nature is one thing and original sin, which inheres [to be innate or inherent] in the corrupted nature and corrupts it, is something else.

1. We believe, teach, and confess that there is a distinction between man's nature and original sin, not only in the beginning when God created man pure and holy and without sin, but also as we now have our nature after the Fall. Even after the fall our nature is and remains a creature of God. The distinction between our nature and original sin is as great as the difference between God's work and the devil's work.

2. We also believe, teach, and confess that we must preserve this distinction most diligently, because the view that admits no distinction between our corrupted human nature and original sin militates against and cannot co-exist with the chief articles of our Christian faith, namely, creation, redemption, sanctification, and the resurrection of our flesh.

God not only created the body and soul of Adam and Eve before the Fall, but also our bodies and souls after the Fall, even though they are corrupted, and God still acknowledges them as his handiwork, as it is written, "Thy hands fashioned and made me, all that I am round about" (Job 10:8).

Furthermore, the Son of God assumed into the unity of His person this same human nature, though without sin, and thus took on Himself not alien flesh, but our own, and according to our flesh has truly become our brother. Hebrews 2:14–17, "Since therefore the children share in flesh and blood, He Himself likewise partook of the same nature. ... For surely it is not with angels that He is concerned but with the descendants of Abraham. Therefore He had to be made like His brethren in every respect," sin excepted.

Thus Christ has redeemed our nature as His creation, sanctifies it as His creation, quickens it from the dead as His creation, and adorns it gloriously as His creation. But He has not created original sin, has not assumed it, has not redeemed it, has not sanctified it, will not quicken it in the elect, will not glorify it or save it. On the contrary, in the resurrection it will be utterly destroyed. These points clearly set forth the distinction between the corrupted nature itself and the corruption which is in the nature and which has corrupted the nature.

3. On the other hand, we believe, teach, and confess that original sin is not a slight corruption of human nature, but that it is so deep a corruption that nothing sound or uncorrupted has survived in man's body or soul, in his inward or outward powers. It is as the church sings, "Through Adam's fall man's nature and essence are all corrupt."

Discussing the Text

1. Describe the distinction between human nature and original sin.

2. Skim Genesis 1:1–31. What is God's "verdict" on His creation? How do the confessors affirm the Word of God?

3. In what ways does the false view of human nature and original sin undermine the work of God?

4. In what ways does the incarnation ["The word made flesh"] affirm human nature?

5. Why do the confessors acknowledge the serious nature of original sin?

6. How does sin affect relationships

    at home?

    at work?

    at school?

    in our neighborhoods and communities?

7. How does original sin contribute to actual sin?

CONNECT

God's Word shows that all people are born in sin—original sin—and that all people live with actual sin daily. We think or say or do something God forbids and fail to think or say or do what God wants. By nature, on our own, we stand condemned—guilty! But God in His love and mercy has shown His grace in Christ. Baptized into His saving death and resurrection, we are forgiven, and holy in His sight.

The Formula of Concord: Solid Declaration

> Although, in Luther's words, original sin, like a spiritual poison and leprosy, has so poisoned and corrupted man's whole nature that within the corrupted nature we are not able to point out and expose the nature by itself and original sin by itself as two manifestly separate things, nevertheless our corrupted nature or the essence of corrupted man, our body and soul or man himself created by God (within which original sin, by which the nature, essence, or total man is corrupted, dwells) are not identical with original sin (which dwells in man's nature or essence and corrupts it). Just as in a case of external leprosy

the body which is leprous and the leprosy on or in the body are not one and the same thing, so, if one wishes to speak strictly, one must maintain a distinction between (a) our nature as it is created and preserved by God and in which sin dwells and (b) original sin itself which dwells in the nature. According to the Holy Scriptures we must and can consider, discuss, and believe these two as distinct from each other.

The chief articles of our Christian faith constrain and compel us to maintain such a distinction. In the first place, in the article of creation Scripture testifies not only that God created human nature before the Fall, but also that after the Fall human nature is God's creature and handiwork (Deuteronomy 32:6; Isaiah 45:11; 54:9; 64:8; Acts 17:25, 26; Revelation 4:11).

These passages indicate clearly that even after the Fall God is man's creator who creates body and soul for him. Therefore the corrupted man cannot be identified unqualifiedly with sin itself, for in that case God would be the creator of sin. In the exposition of the First Article of the Creed in the Small Catechism we confess, "I believe that God has created *me* and all that exists, that He has given me and still sustains my body and soul, eyes, ears, and all my members, my reason and all my senses." Similarly we confess in the Large Catechism, "I hold and believe that I am a creature of God; that is, that He has given and constantly sustains my body, soul, and life, my members great and small, all the faculties of my mind, my reason and understanding," etc. It is of course true that this creature and handiwork of God has been miserably corrupted by sin, for the dough out of which God forms and makes man has been corrupted and prevented in Adam and is transmitted to us in this condition. At this point all Christian hearts may well ponder God's inexpressible kindness in that He does not immediately cast this corrupted, perverted, and sinful dough into hell-fire, but out of it He makes and fashions our present human nature, which is so miserable corrupted by sin, in order that through His beloved Son He might cleanse it from sin, sanctify it, and save it. This article shows the difference irrefutably and clearly, because original sin does not come from God, nor is God the creator or author of sin. Neither is original sin the creature or handiwork of God; on the contrary, it is the devil's work. (Article 1, sections 33–34, 38–40)

1. How does Luther's illustration serve to clarify the distinction between original sin and human nature?

2. In what ways does our creation and redemption in Christ bring genuine and lasting self-worth?

3. Describe how the Gospel affirms and dignifies our daily existence.

4. What encouragement do you have for eternity as God's baptized child *today*?

VISION

Personal Reflection

1. Luther used leprosy as an example to distinguish between original sin and human nature. What parallel can you create to explain the same concept?
2. What would you say to a fellow Christian who says, "Since I'm afflicted with original sin, I won't even try to obey God's will"?
3. Why does original sin give you reason to thank God rather than criticize Him for your condition?

Family Connection

1. Think of one way your family can together fight a specific result of human sin in our world. Ask God for His mercy and strength as you carry out your plan.
2. Locate and examine your baptismal certificates. Were you baptized as an infant? Why did you need Baptism even before you could consciously sin? Ask a younger family member to make up a prayer thanking God for Baptism.
3. Talk with children about the excitement that surrounded

their birth. Remind children that God creates life and that He loves us so much that He took away our sins through Christ.

Closing Worship

Sing or read together "Jesus Sinners Will Receive" (*LW* 229).

Jesus sinners will receive;
May they all this saying ponder
Who in sin's delusions live
And from God and heaven wander!
Here is hope for all who grieve:
Jesus sinners will receive.

We deserve but grief and shame,
Yet His words, rich grace revealing,
Pardon, peace, and life proclaim.
Here our ills have perfect healing;
We with humble hearts believe
Jesus sinners will receive

Jesus sinners will receive.
Even me He has forgiven;
And when I this earth must leave,
I shall find an open heaven.
Dying, still to Him I cleave—
Jesus sinners will receive.

For Next Week

Read Article 2 of the Formula of Concord (Epitome).

Article 2

FOCUS

Theme: Free Will

Law/Gospel Focus

Unregenerated men and women are sinners and enemies of God. The Holy Spirit alone brings forgiveness and new life through the Gospel and sacraments. We confess who we are—sinners—and rejoice in what God has made us to be: saints, alive, by grace alone in Jesus Christ.

Objectives

By the power of the Holy Spirit working through God's Word, we will

1. understand the truth of God's Word on our human condition apart from God;
2. acknowledge and repent of our sinfulness and trust in Christ as the only Savior;
3. rejoice in God's regeneration of His people through Word and Sacrament.

Opening Worship

Read together these words from 1 Corinthians 2 as a responsive prayer.

Leader: We do, however, speak a message of wisdom among the mature, but not the wisdom of this age or of the rulers of this age, who are coming to nothing.

Participants: No, we speak of God's secret wisdom, a wisdom that has been hidden and that God destined for our glory before time began.

Leader: None of the rulers of this age understood it, for if they had, they would not have crucified the Lord of glory.

Participants: However, as it is written: "No eye has seen, no ear has heard, no mind has conceived what God has prepared for those who love Him."

Leader: But God has revealed it to us by His Spirit. The Spirit searches all things, even the deep things of God.

Participant: We have not received the Spirit of the world but the Spirit who is from God, that we may understand what God has freely given us.

Introduction

Do we choose to believe in Christ? After Luther's death, some evangelicals answered yes! The issue remains today. A brother or sister in Christ asserts, "I gave my heart to Jesus." Preachers insist, "You must decide for Christ!" The Formula of Concord addresses the controversy squarely in Article 2.

1. In what ways is freedom cherished by people of the world?

2. Why do people insist on a "free will" in spiritual matters?

INFORM

The Formula of Concord: Epitome

The will of man may be discussed in four different states: (1) before the Fall, (2) after the Fall, (3) after regeneration, (4) after the resurrection of the flesh. In this controversy the primary question revolves exclusively about man's will and ability in the second state. The question is, What powers does man possess in spiritual matters after the fall of our first parents and before his regeneration? Can man by his own powers, before he is reborn through the Holy Spirit, dispose and prepare himself for the grace of God? Can he or can he not accept the grace of God offered in the Word and the holy sacraments?

1. It is our teaching, faith, and confession that in spiritual matters man's understanding and reason are blind and that he understands nothing by his own powers, as it is written in 1 Corinthians 2:14, "The unspiritual man does not receive the gifts of the Spirit of God, for they are folly to him, and he is not able to understand them" when he is examined concerning spiritual things.

2. Likewise we believe, teach, and confess that man's unregenerated will is not only turned away from God, but has also become an enemy of God, so that he desires and wills only that which is evil and opposed to God, as it is written, "The imagination of man's heart is evil from his youth" [Genesis 8:21]. Likewise, "The mind that is set on the flesh is hostile to God; it does not submit to God's law, indeed it cannot" [Romans 8:7]. As little as a corpse can quicken itself to bodily, earthly life, so little can man who through sin is spiritually dead raise himself to spiritual life, as it is written, "When we were dead through our trespasses, He made us alive together with Christ" [Ephesians 2:5]. Therefore we are not of ourselves "sufficient to claim anything as coming from us; our sufficiency is from God" (2 Corinthians 3:5).

3. God the Holy Spirit, however, does not effect conversion without means; He employs to this end the preaching and the hearing of God's Word, as it is written that the Gospel is a "power of God" for salvation [Romans 1:16]; likewise, that faith comes from the hearing of God's Word (Romans 10:17). It is God's will that men should hear His Word and not stop their ears [Psalm 95:8]. The Holy Spirit is present with this Word and

opens hearts so that, like Lydia in Acts 16:14, they heed it and thus are converted solely through the grace and power of the Holy Spirit, for man's conversion is the Spirit's work alone. Without His grace our "will and effort" [Romans 9:16], our planting, sowing, and watering are in vain unless He "gives the growth" [1 Corinthians 3:7]. Christ also states, "Apart from Me you can do nothing" [John 15:5]. In these few words He denies all power to free will and ascribes everything to the grace of God, so that no one might boast in the presence of God (1 Corinthians 9:16).

Discussing the Text

1. Describe our condition apart from God's saving work in Christ.

2. What evidence do you see today that, by nature, people are opposed to God?

3. How does the analogy of the corpse help to picture unregenerated humankind?

4. What means does the Spirit use to "make alive"?

5. Explain—and apply—the Lord's words: "Apart from Me you can do nothing."

6. In what ways could free will in spiritual matters open the door to boasting?

7. Why did the confessors deny *all* power to the human will in spiritual matters?

CONNECT

Human beings cannot believe in Jesus by our own strength or mental activity. We rightfully attribute our entire conversion to the Holy Spirit, who has called us by the Gospel and who continues to sanctify us.

The Formula of Concord: Solid Declaration

In order to settle this controversy in a Christian way according to the Word of God, and by God's grace to bring it to an end, we submit the following as our teaching, belief, and confession: We believe that in spiritual and divine things the intellect, heart, and will of unregenerated man cannot by any native or natural powers in any way understand, believe, accept, imagine, will, begin, accomplish, do, effect, or cooperate, but that man is entirely and completely dead and corrupted as far as anything good is concerned. Accordingly, we believe that after the Fall and prior to his conversion not a spark of spiritual powers has remained or exists in man by which he could make himself ready for the grace of God or to accept the proffered grace, nor that he has any capacity for grace by and for himself or can apply himself to it or prepare himself for it, or help, do, effect, or cooperate toward his conversion by his own powers, either altogether or half-way or in the tiniest or smallest degree, "of himself as coming from himself," but is a slave of sin (John 8:34), the captive of the devil who drives him (Ephesians 2:2; 2 Timothy 2:26). Hence according to its perverse disposition and nature the natural free will is mighty and active only in the direction of that which is displeasing and contrary to God.

Thus Scripture denies to the intellect, heart, and will of the natural man every capacity, aptitude, skill, and ability to think anything good or right in spiritual matters, to understand them, to begin them, to will them, to undertake them, to do them, to accomplish or to cooperate in them as of himself. "Not that we are sufficient of ourselves to claim anything as coming from us; our sufficiency is from God" (2 Corinthians 3:5). "They are all incompetent" (Romans 3:12). "My Word finds no place in you" (John 8:37). "The darkness comprehended it not" (John 1:5). "The unspiritual man does not receive (or, as the Greek word actually has it, does not grasp, take hold of, or apprehend) the gifts of the Spirit of God (that is, he has no capacity for spiritual things) for they are folly to him, and he is not able to understand them" (1 Corinthians 2:14). Much less will he be able truly to believe the Gospel, give his assent to it, and accept it as truth. For the mind that is set on the flesh (the natural man's understanding) "is hostile to God; it does not submit to God's law, indeed it cannot" (Romans 8:7). Summing up everything, what the Son of God says remains eternally true, "Apart from Me you can do nothing" (John 15:5), and what St. Paul says is also true, "For God is at work in you, both to will and to work for His good pleasure" (Philippians 2:13). This appealing passage is of very great comfort to all devout Christians who perceive and discover a little spark and a longing for the grace of God and eternal salvation in their hearts. They know that God, who has kindled this beginning of true godliness in their heart, wills to continue to support them in their great weakness and to help them to remain in true faith until their end. (Article 2, sections 6–7, 12–14)

1. How does the confessors' position magnify the grace and power of God?

2. In what ways is the Gospel still "foolishness" in our world?

3. Describe how your "sufficiency" is found in Christ alone.

4. "God, who has kindled this beginning of true godliness in their heart, wills to continue to support ... and to help them. ..." What comfort do you have in knowing God is at work today in your life?

VISION

Personal Reflection

1. How did you become a believer?
2. How does your daily life confirm both sinfulness and your faith?

Family Connection

1. The same Word that brought you to faith remains a necessary nutrient of your active faith. Plan regular family devotions. Use resources that are appropriate for the younger members of your family. Ask your pastor to recommend family devotional material.
2. While you cannot cooperate on your own conversion, you can strive to *serve* Christ after you come to faith. What can you do to serve the Lord within worship? Within your home? With neighbors? At work or school?

Closing Worship

Sing or pray together "Holy Spirit, Light Divine" (*LW* 166).

Holy Spirit, light divine,
Dawn up on this soul of mine;
Let Your word dispel the night,
Wake my spirit, clear my sight.

Holy Spirit, grace divine,
Cleanse this sinful heart of mine;
In Your mercy look on me,
From sin's bondage set me free.

Holy Spirit, peace divine,
Still this restless heart of mine;
Speak to calm the tossing sea,
Stayed in Your tranquility.

For Next Week

Read Article 3 of the Formula of Concord (Epitome).

Article 3

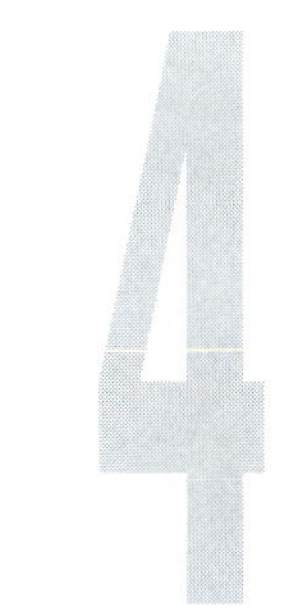

FOCUS

Theme: The Righteousness of Faith before God

Law/Gospel Focus

All people, sinful from birth, are justified before God and saved solely in Christ, so that Christ alone is our righteousness. Without Christ as our righteousness we stand before God only as "lost and condemned creatures." But by God's grace, through faith, we receive the blessings of His saving work: forgiveness, life, and salvation.

Objectives

By the power of the Holy Spirit working through God's Word, we will

1. understand why the *whole* Christ is our righteousness before God;
2. acknowledge our own "righteousness"—none at all—in the light of God's holy Law;
3. live in the righteousness that is ours only through faith in Jesus Christ.

Opening Worship

Read together these words from 1 Corinthians 3 as a responsive prayer.

Leader: What, after all, is Apollos? And what is Paul? Only servants, through whom you came to believe—as the Lord has assigned to each his task.
Participants: I planted the seed, Apollos watered it, but God made it grow.
Leader: So neither he who plants nor he who waters is anything, but only God, who makes things grow.
Participants: The man who plants and the man who waters have one purpose, and each will be rewarded according to his own labor.
Leader: For we are God's fellow workers; you are God's field, God's building.
Participants: By the grace God has given me, I laid a foundation as an expert builder, and someone else is building on it.
Leader: But each one should be careful how he builds.
Participants: For no one can lay any foundation other than the one already laid, which is Jesus Christ.

Introduction

"Saved, by grace, in Christ." This truth is the central article in faith of the Christian church. Yet shortly after Luther's death the Lutherans disagreed among themselves on this issue.

The trouble began when Andrew Osiander began to teach that our righteousness before God does not come from being *pronounced* righteous, but by *becoming* righteous gradually, progressively through the indwelling of the Son of God in us by faith.

Both Melanchthon and Flacius opposed Osiander's view. They correctly perceived that Osiander was making the *effect* of justification into its *cause.*

Others added to the problem by teaching that it was only the human nature of Christ, not the divine, that was involved in acquiring our redemption. Article 3 of the Formula of Concord presents the truth of God's Word.

1. How do people generally regard the phrase "right with God"?

2. What problems do you see with the idea that we become righteous *gradually* before God?

INFORM

The Formula of Concord: Epitome

It is the unanimous confession of our churches according to the Word of God and the content of the Augsburg Confession that we poor sinners are justified before God and saved solely by faith in Christ, so that Christ alone is our righteousness. He is truly God and man since in Him the divine and human natures are personally united to one another (Jeremiah 23:6; 1 Corinthians 1:30; 2 Corinthians 5:21). Because of the foregoing a question has arisen, According to which nature is Christ our righteousness? ...

1. We believe, teach, and confess unanimously that Christ is our righteousness neither according to the divine nature alone nor according to the human nature alone. On the contrary, the entire Christ according to both natures is our righteousness solely in His obedience which as God and man He rendered to His heavenly Father into death itself. Thereby He won for us in the forgiveness of sins and eternal life, as it is written, "For as by one man's disobedience many were made sinners, so by *one man's obedience* many will be made righteous" (Romans 5:19).

2. Accordingly we believe, teach, and confess that our righteousness before God consists in this, that God forgives us our sins purely by His grace, without any preceding, present, or subsequent work, merit, or worthiness, and reckons to us the righteousness of Christ's obedience, on account of which righteousness we are accepted by God into grace and are regarded as righteous.

3. We believe, teach, and confess that faith is the only means and instrument whereby we accept Christ and in Christ obtain

the "righteousness which avails before God," and that for Christ's sake such faith is reckoned for righteousness (Romans 4:5).

4. We believe, teach, and confess that this faith is not a mere knowledge of the stories about Christ, but the kind of gift of God by which in the Word of the Gospel we recognize Christ aright as our redeemer and trust in Him, so that solely because of His obedience, by grace, we have forgiveness of sins, are regarded as holy and righteous by God the Father, and shall be saved eternally.

5. We believe, teach, and confess that according to the usage of Scripture the word "justify" means in this article "absolve," that is, pronounce free from sin. "He who justifies the wicked and he who condemns the righteous are both alike an abomination to the Lord" (Proverbs 17:15); likewise, "Who shall bring any charge against God's elect? It is God who justifies" (Romans 8:33). Sometimes, as in the Apology, the words *regeneratio* (rebirth) and *vivificatio* (making alive) are used in place of justification, and then they mean the same thing, even though otherwise these terms refer to the renovation of man and distinguish it from justification by faith.

6. We also believe, teach, and confess that, although the genuinely believing and truly regenerated persons retain much weakness and many shortcomings down to their graves, they still have no reason to doubt either the righteousness which is reckoned to them through faith or the salvation of their souls, but they must regard it as certain that for Christ's sake, on the basis of the promises and the Word of the holy Gospel, they have a gracious God.

7. We believe, teach, and confess that if we would preserve the pure doctrine concerning the righteousness of faith before God, we must give special attention to the "exclusive terms," that is, to those words of the holy apostle Paul which separate the merit of Christ completely from our own works and give all glory to Christ alone. Thus the holy apostle Paul uses such expressions as *"by grace,"* "without merit," "without the law," "without works," "not by works," etc. All these expressions say in effect that we become righteous and are saved "alone by faith" in Christ.

8. We believe, teach, and confess that the contrition that precedes justification and the good works that follow it do not belong in the article of justification before God. Nevertheless,

we should not imagine a kind of faith in this connection that could coexist and co-persist with a wicked intention to sin and to act contrary to one's conscience. On the contrary, after a person has been justified by faith, a true living faith becomes "active through love" (Galatians 5:6). Thus good works always follow justifying faith and are certainly to be found with it, since such faith is never alone but is always accompanied by love and hope.

Discussing the Text

1. Summarize the "main doctrine" of our faith.

2. Describe the two natures of Christ. How are both natures involved in His saving work?

3. In what ways do the confessors exclude all human effort or works from salvation?

4. Explain the statement "Faith is the only means and instrument whereby we accept Christ."

5. How is faith rooted in knowledge? How is faith more than knowledge?

6. Define *justify*. What words and illustration help you to understand justification by grace through faith?

7. Why is the distinction between *being declared righteous* and *becoming righteous* important to God's people?

CONNECT

The concept of justification and righteousness, as the confessors understood it, does not make sense to some people. They struggle with the paradox that while we are righteous before God for Jesus' sake, we still sin and struggle with some very unrighteous thoughts and deeds. Yet Jesus' death and resurrection have justified us completely. The key to understanding this lies not in human reason, but only in trusting God's Word as revealed in Holy Scripture.

The Formula of Concord: Solid Declaration

Hence, since in our churches the theologians of the Augsburg Confession accept the principle that we must seek our entire righteousness apart from our own and all other human merits, works, virtues, and worthiness and that our righteousness rests solely and alone on the Lord Christ, it is important to consider carefully in what way Christ is called our righteousness in this matter of justification: Our righteousness rests neither upon His divine nature nor upon His human nature but upon the entire person of Christ, who as God and man in His sole, total, and perfect obedience is our righteousness.

For even though Christ had been conceived by the Holy Spirit without sin and had been born and had in His human nature alone fulfilled all righteousness but had not been true, eternal God, the obedience and passion of the human nature could not be reckoned to us as righteousness. Likewise, if the Son of God had not become man, the divine nature alone could not have been our righteousness. Therefore we believe, teach, and confess that the total obedience of Christ's total person, which He rendered to His heavenly Father even to the most ignominious death of the cross, is reckoned to us as righteousness. For neither the obedience nor the passion of the human nature alone, without the divine nature, could render satisfaction to the eternal and almighty God for the sins of all the world. Likewise, the deity alone, without the humanity, could not mediate between God and us.

Since, as was mentioned above, it is the obedience of the entire person, therefore it is a perfect satisfaction and reconciliation of the human race, since it satisfied the eternal and immutable [changeless] righteousness of God revealed in the law. This obedience is our righteousness which avails before God and is revealed in the Gospel, upon which faith depends before God and which God reckons to faith, as it is written, "For as by one man's disobedience many will be made sinners, so by one man's obedience many will be made righteous" (Romans 5:19), and "the blood of Jesus, His Son, cleanses us from all sin" (1 John 1:7), and again, "The righteous shall live by his faith" (Habakkuk 2:4). (Article 3, sections 55–57)

1. In what ways does faith in Christ, our fully divine and fully human Savior, strengthen you to live today?

2. Describe how Christ's work is the "*perfect* satisfaction and reconciliation of the human race."

3. How does a proper understanding of justification bring comfort and certainty to God's people?

VISION

Personal Reflection

1. How would your life be different if you lived 100 percent under the conviction that Christ's righteousness *alone* saves you?
2. Reflect on the comfort, assurance, and encouragement you receive from knowing that when the Gospel is preached, the Holy Spirit is working faith in your heart and in the hearts of His people, the church.
3. Had you lived at the time of Christ, what in His life would have been evidence of His true human nature? His true divine nature?

Family Connection

1. Draw a Good Friday picture and an Easter picture. Discuss why both events were necessary to save us.
2. Gather several tools for a "tool talk." Slip a cross (hand drawn is okay) in with the tools. Ask children how each tool can be used both to destroy and to build. Ask how God used the cross both to destroy and to build.
3. Prepare a small gift for each family member. Give the gifts, attaching to them no significant day or event. When recipients ask why they received the gift, tell them it's simply a gift of love—just as God sent Jesus because He loved us.

Closing Worship

Sing or pray together "By Grace I'm Saved" (*LW* 351).

By grace I'm saved, grace free and boundless;
My soul, believe and doubt it not.
Why stagger at this word of promise?
Has Scripture ever falsehood taught?
No; then this word must true remain:
By grace you too will life obtain.

By grace God's Son, our only Savior,
Came down to earth to bear our sin.
Was it because of your own merit
That Jesus died your soul to win?
No, it was grace, and grace alone,
That brought Him from His heav'nly throne.

By grace! On this I'll rest when dying;
In Jesus' promise I rejoice;
For though I know my heart's condition,
I also know my Savior's voice.
My heart is glad, all grief has flown
Since I am saved by grace alone.

For Next Week

Read Article 4 of the Formula of Concord (Epitome).

Article 4

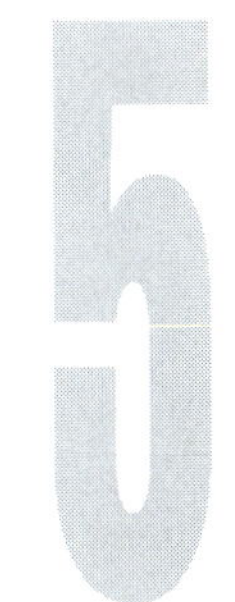

FOCUS

Theme: Good Works

Law/Gospel Focus

We are saved by grace through faith in Jesus Christ, not by works. Yet faith without works is dead. Because of sin, we desire to be justified by what we do, or we resist the work of the Holy Spirit to renew and conform us to the image of Christ. Yet forgiven in our Baptism and restored daily by God's mercy in Jesus, we are strengthened to serve the Savior and one another.

Objectives

By the power of the Holy Spirit working through God's Word, we will

1. understand the teaching of God's Word on faith and good works in our lives;
2. repent of our failures to live as God's forgiven and renewed people;
3. thank God for the work of the Spirit to bring us daily to Christ through Word and Sacrament.

Opening Worship

Read together these words from 1 Corinthians 13 as a responsive prayer.

Leader: Love is patient, love is kind. It does not envy, it does not boast, it is not proud. It is not rude, it is not self-seeking, it is not easily angered, it keeps no record of wrongs.
Participants: Love does not delight in evil but rejoices with the truth. It always protects, always trusts, always hopes, always perseveres.
Leader: Love never fails. But where there are prophecies, they will cease; where there are tongues, they will be stilled; where there is knowledge, it will pass away.
Participants: For we know in part and we prophesy in part, but when perfection comes, the imperfect disappears.
Leader: When I was a child, I talked like a child, I thought like a child, I reasoned like a child. When I became a man, I put childish ways behind me.
Participants: Now we see but a poor reflection as in a mirror; then we shall see face to face. Now I know in part; then I shall know fully, even as I am fully known.
Leader: And now these three remain: faith, hope and love.
Participants: But the greatest of these is love.

Introduction

Controversy in the Lutheran church concerning the role of good works in the Christian life was severe. Both John Major, who would become president of Wittenburg University after Luther's death, and Philip Melanchthon persisted in using such language as "good works are necessary to salvation." In an incautious attempt to counter such language, Nicholas Amsdorf suggested that good works were actually injurious to salvation! John Agricola suggested that good works should not be spoken of at all and that the Law had no further place in the life of the Christian. To resolve these questions, Article 4 focuses on God's Word about faith and works.

1. For what reasons might someone claim the necessity of good works for salvation?

2. What do you think of when you hear the phrase "good works"?

INFORM

The Formula of Concord: Epitome

In order to explain this controversy from the ground up and to resolve it, this is our doctrine, faith, and confession:

1. That good works, like fruits of a good tree, certainly and indubitably follow genuine faith—if it is a living and not a dead faith.

2. We believe, teach, and confess that good works should be completely excluded from a discussion of the article of man's salvation as well as from the article of our justification before God. The Apostle affirms in clear terms, "So also David declares that salvation pertains only to the man to whom God reckons righteousness apart from works, saying, 'Blessed are those whose iniquities are forgiven, and whose sins are covered'" (Romans 4:6–8). And again, "For by grace you have been saved through faith; and this is not your own doing, it is the gift of God—not because of works, lest any man should boast" (Ephesians 2:8–9).

3. We believe, teach, and confess further that all men, but especially those who are regenerated and renewed by the Holy Spirit, are obligated to do good works.

4. In this sense the words "necessary," "ought," and "must" are correctly and in a Christian way applied to the regenerated and are in no way contrary to the pattern of sound words and terminology.

5. However, when applied to the regenerated the words "necessity" and "necessary" are to be understood as involving not coercion but the due obedience which genuine believers, in so far as they are reborn, render not by coercion or compulsion

of the law but from a spontaneous spirit because they are "no longer under the law but under grace" [Romans 6:14; 7:6; 8:14].

6. Therefore we also believe, teach, and confess that the statement, "The regenerated do good works from a free spirit," should not be understood as though it were left to the regenerated person's option whether to do or not to do good and that he might keep his faith even if he deliberately were to persist in sin.

7. This, however, should be understood exactly as our Lord and the apostles themselves explain it, as applying only to the liberated spirit which does good works not from a fear of punishment, like a slave, but out of a love of righteousness, like a child (Romans 8:15).

8. However, in the elect children of God this spontaneity is not perfect, but they are still encumbered with much weakness, as St. Paul complains of himself in Romans 7:14–25 and Galatians 5:17.

9. Nevertheless, for Christ's sake the Lord does not reckon this weakness against His elect, as it is written, "There is therefore now no condemnation for those who are in Christ Jesus" (Romans 8:1).

10. We also believe, teach, and confess that not our works but only the Holy Spirit, working through faith, preserves faith and salvation in us. The good works are testimonies of the Holy Spirit's presence and indwelling.

Discussing the Text

1. Summarize our teaching about good works in the life of the Christian.

2. What false assumptions and teachings does Article 4 address?

3. Describe a "genuine," "living" faith.

4. In what sense are *all* people—under God's *Law*— obligated to do good works?

5. In what sense are *God's* people—under the *Gospel*—obligated to do good works?

6. Respond: "Christians have to do good works."

7. Describe the difference between a response under slavery and as a beloved child.

8. How do the confessors anchor good works in faith and the Holy Spirit?

CONNECT

Christians come to faith by the Word working through the power of the Holy Spirit. We need not and cannot do anything to acquire faith and salvation. Yet once saved, God's people blossom with good works because God has been so good to us. We rejoice in His mercy in Christ and seek to do His will.

The Formula of Concord: Solid Declaration

> First of all, there is in this article no disagreement among us concerning the following points: That it is God's will, ordinance, and command that believers walk in good works; that only those are truly good works which God Himself prescribes and commands in His Word, and not those that an individual may devise according to his own opinion or that are based on human traditions; that truly good works are not done by a person's own natural powers but only after a person has been reconciled to God through faith and renewed through the Holy Spirit, or, as St. Paul says, "has been created in Christ Jesus for good works."

Hence faith alone is the mother and source of the truly good and God-pleasing works that God will reward both in this and in the next world. For this reason St. Paul calls them fruits of faith or of the Spirit.

For, as Luther writes in his Preface of Epistle of St. Paul to the Romans, "Faith is a divine work in us that transforms us and begets us anew from God, kills the Old Adam, makes us entirely different people in heart, spirit, mind, and all our powers, and brings the Holy Spirit with it. Oh, faith is a living, busy, active, mighty thing, so that it is impossible for it not to be constantly doing what is good. Likewise, faith does not ask if good works are to be done, but before one can ask, faith has already done them and is constantly active. Whoever does not perform such good works is a faithless man, blindly tapping around in search of faith and good works without knowing what either faith or good works are, and in the meantime he chatters and jabbers a great deal about faith and good works. Faith is a vital, deliberate trust in God's grace, so certain that it would die a thousand times for it. And such confidence and knowledge of divine grace makes us joyous, mettlesome, and merry toward God and all creatures. This the Holy Spirit works by faith, and therefore without any coercion a man is willing and desirous to do good to everyone, to serve everyone, to suffer everything for the love of God and to His glory, who has been so gracious to him. It is therefore as impossible to separate works from faith as it is to separate heat and light from fire." (Article 5, sections 7, 9–12)

1. In what ways are you thankful that God calls, strengthens, and equips you to do good works?

2. "Faith is a living, busy, active, mighty thing." Explain.

3. Why is it important to rely on God's Word for guidance, rather than our human opinions and ideas?

4. How can those who do good works remain humble about their deeds?

VISION

Personal Reflection

1. We often think more about doing good works than receiving them. Who has done godly good works for you? What happens when others do good for you?
2. Think of several Bible passages that comfort you and bring you joy. Look them up. Do the verses preceding or following your favorite passages suggest good works in response to God's love? What specifically can you do in response to your favorite passages?

Family Connection

1. Discuss ways that your family can work together on behalf of the poor.
2. Adopt a family mission project for one to three months. Take a weekly or daily "collection" to make a monetary gift. (Monetary gifts need not be large.) Pray for the mission and the missionaries. Write to them. Ask your pastor to suggest appropriate missions or adopt a local one.
3. Volunteer as a family for community service. Consider regular cleaning of an area near your home or apartment. Bake brownies for the local fire department or pray for police officers. Plan what you will say when others thank you for your service.

Closing Worship

Sing or pray together "God of Grace and God of Glory" (*LW* 398).

God of grace and God of glory,
On Your people pour Your pow'r;
Crown Your ancient church's story;
Bring its bud to glorious flow'r.
Grant us wisdom, grant us courage
For the facing of this hour,
For the facing of this hour.

Cure Your children's warring madness;
Bend our pride to Your control;
Shame our wanton, selfish gladness,
Rich in things and poor in soul.
Grant us wisdom, grant us courage
Lest we miss Your kingdom's goal,
Lest we miss Your kingdom's goal.

Save us from weak resignation
To the evils we deplore;
Let the gift of Your salvation
Be our glory evermore.
Grant us wisdom, grant us courage,
Serving You whom we adore,
Serving You whom we adore.

For Next Week

Read Article 5 of the Formula of Concord (Epitome).

Article 5

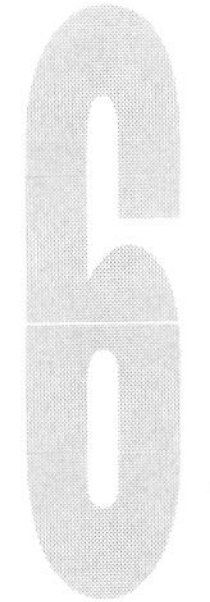

FOCUS

Theme: Law and Gospel

Law/Gospel Focus

In His Word, God speaks His Law and His Gospel. By nature, we confuse God's judgment and grace; we fail to distinguish between what God demands of us and what He has done for us in Christ. Forgiven in Jesus, the Spirit leaves us with the comfort and hope of the Gospel of eternal life and salvation.

Objectives

By the power of the Holy Spirit working through God's Word, we will

1. understand the difference between God's Law and Gospel and how both terms are used in Scripture;
2. know the heart of the Gospel (in contrast to the Law): the forgiveness of sins, life, and salvation;
3. live as people freed and renewed by the Gospel.

Opening Worship

Read together these words from 2 Corinthians 1 as a responsive prayer.

Leader: Praise be to the God and Father of our Lord Jesus Christ, the Father of compassion and the God of all comfort,

Participants: Who comforts us in all our troubles, so that we can comfort those in any trouble with the comfort we ourselves have received from God.

Leader: For just as the sufferings of Christ flow over into our lives, so also through Christ our comfort overflows.

Participants: If we are distressed, it is for your comfort and salvation;

Leader: If we are comforted, it is for your comfort, which produces in you patient endurance of the same sufferings we suffer.

Participants: And our hope for you is firm, because we know that just as you share in our sufferings, so also you share in our comfort.

Introduction

According to John Agricola, a colleague of both Luther and Melanchthon, the Law had little role to play in the regenerated person's life. Although Luther was able to get Agricola to moderate his views, this was no longer possible after Luther's death. Melanchthon, too, allowed that the preaching of the Gospel could include urging contrition, as well as a condemnation of sin. But Melanchthon was also using "Gospel" in its widest sense, which Scripture itself supports. Melanchthon never believed that repentance was the work of the Gospel. Instead, he rightly taught that it was the function of the Law to bring forth repentance.

To help pastors and laypeople distinguish between Law and Gospel, the confessors confessed the truth of God's Word in Article 5.

1. Give several examples of "Law" from the Bible.

2. Give several examples of "Gospel" from the Bible.

3. In what ways is it difficult to distinguish Law and Gospel?

INFORM

The Formula of Concord: Epitome

The question has been, Is the preaching of the Holy Gospel strictly speaking only a preaching of grace which proclaims the forgiveness of sins, or is it also a preaching of repentance and reproof that condemns unbelief, since unbelief is condemned not in the law but wholly through the Gospel?

1. We believe, teach, and confess that the distinction between law and Gospel is an especially glorious light that is to be maintained with great diligence in the church so that, according to St. Paul's admonition, the Word of God may be divided rightly.

2. We believe, teach, and confess that, strictly speaking, the law is a divine doctrine which teaches what is right and God-pleasing and which condemns everything that is sinful and contrary to God's will.

3. Therefore everything which condemns sin is and belongs to the proclamation of the law.

4. But the Gospel, strictly speaking, is the kind of doctrine that teaches what a man who has not kept the law and is condemned by it should believe, namely, that Christ has satisfied and paid for all guilt and without man's merit has obtained and won for him forgiveness of sins, the "righteousness that avails before God" [Romans 1:17; 2 Corinthians 5:21], and eternal life.

5. The word "Gospel" is not used in a single sense in Holy Scripture, and this was the original occasion of the controversy. Therefore we believe, teach, and confess that when the word "Gospel" means the entire doctrine of Christ which He proclaimed personally in His teaching ministry and which His apostles also set forth (examples of this meaning occur in Mark

1:15 and Acts 20:24), then it is correct to say or write that the Gospel is a proclamation both of repentance and of forgiveness of sins.

6. But when the law and Gospel are opposed to each other, as when Moses is spoken of as a teacher of the law in contrast to Christ as a preacher of the Gospel, then we believe, teach, and confess that the Gospel is not a proclamation of contrition and reproof but is, strictly speaking, precisely a comforting and joyful message which does not reprove or terrify but comforts consciences that are frightened by the law, directs them solely to the merit of Christ, and raises them up again by the delightful proclamation of God's grace and favor acquired through the merits of Christ.

7. Now as to the disclosure of sin, as long as men hear only the law and hear nothing about Christ, the veil of Moses [2 Corinthians 3:13–16] covers their eyes, as a result they fail to learn the true nature of sin from the law, and thus they become either conceited hypocrites, like the Pharisees, or they despair, as Judas did, etc. Therefore Christ takes the law into His own hands and explains it spiritually (Matthew 5:21–48; Romans 7:14). Then "God's wrath is revealed from heaven" over all sinners [Romans 1:18] and men learn how fierce it is. Thus they are directed back to the law, and now they learn from it for the first time the real nature of their sin, an acknowledgment which Moses could never have wrung from them.

Therefore the proclamation of the suffering and death of Christ, the Son of God, is an earnest and terrifying preaching and advertisement of God's wrath which really directs people into the law, after the veil of Moses has been removed for them, so they now know for the first time what great things God demands of us in the law, none of which we could fulfill, and that we should now seek all our righteousness in Christ.

8. Nevertheless, as long as all this—namely, the passion and death of Christ—proclaims God's wrath and terrifies people, it is not, strictly speaking, the preaching of the Gospel but the preaching of Moses and the law, and therefore it is an "alien work" [Isaiah 28:21] of Christ by which He comes to His proper office—namely, to preach grace, to comfort, to make alive. And this is the preaching of the Gospel, strictly speaking.

Discussing the Text

1. Why did the confessors label the subject of Law and Gospel "an especially glorious light"?

2. What is God's Law? What does it do?

3. How do people generally view God's Word as Law?

4. What is the Gospel? Describe what the Gospel does for human beings.

5. How are Law and Gospel different? Why is it important to keep this vast difference?

6. What often happens when we mix the Law with the Gospel?

7. Are there any situations where we could proclaim the Law without proclaiming the Gospel and vice versa? Why or why not?

CONNECT

All people need to know their sinful nature and the consequences of sin; this knowledge, in turn, reveals their need for a Savior. God's salvation is shown in the unconditional love of Christ. How unconditional is His love? Paul writes,

"God demonstrates His own love for us in this: While we were still sinners, Christ died for us" (Romans 5:8). Paul confessed both Law and Gospel when he said, "Here is a trustworthy saying that deserves full acceptance: Christ Jesus came into the world to save sinners—of whom I am the worst" (1 Timothy 1:15). We are free and blessed to adopt Paul's words as our own.

The Formula of Concord: Solid Declaration

> We unanimously believe, teach, and confess on the basis of what we have said that, strictly speaking, the law is a divine doctrine which reveals the righteousness and immutable [changeless] will of God, shows how man ought to be disposed in his nature, thoughts, words, and deeds in order to be pleasing and acceptable to God, and threatens the transgressors of the law with God's wrath and temporal and eternal punishment. ...
>
> The Gospel, however, is that doctrine which teaches what a man should believe in order to obtain the forgiveness of sins from God, since man has failed to keep the law of God and has transgressed it, his corrupted nature, thoughts, words, and deeds war against the law, and he is therefore subject to the wrath of God, to death, to temporal miseries, and to the punishment of hell-fire. The content of the Gospel is this, that the Son of God, Christ our Lord, Himself assumed and bore the curse of the law and expiated [made amends for] and paid for all our sins, that through Him alone we re-enter the good graces of God, obtain forgiveness of sins through faith, are freed from death and all the punishments of sin, and are saved eternally. For everything which comforts and which offers the mercy and grace of God to transgressors of the law strictly speaking is, and is called, the Gospel, a good and joyful message that God wills not to punish sins but to forgive them for Christ's sake.
>
> Accordingly every penitent sinner must believe—that is, he must put his confidence solely on the Lord Jesus Christ, "who was put to death for our trespasses and raised for our justification" [Romans 4:25], who "was made sin though He knew no sin, so that in Him we might become the righteousness of God" [2 Corinthians 5:21], who was "made our righteousness" [1 Corinthians 1:30], and whose obedience is reckoned to us as righteousness in the strict judgment of God. ...

We believe and confess that these two doctrines must be urged constantly and diligently in the church of God until the end of the world, but with the due distinction, so that in the ministry of the New Testament the proclamation of the law and its threats will terrify the hearts of the unrepentant and bring them to a knowledge of their sin and to repentance, but not in such a way that they become despondent and despair therein. Rather, since "the law was our custodian until Christ came, that we might be justified by faith" (Galatians 3:24), and hence points and leads not away from but toward the Christ who is the end of the law (Romans 10:4), the proclamation of the Gospel of our Lord Christ will once more comfort and strengthen them with the assurance that if they believe that Gospel God forgives them all their sins through Christ, accepts them for His sake as God's children, and out of pure grace, without any merit of their own, justifies and saves them. But this does not mean that men may abuse the grace of God and sin against grace. This distinction between the law and the Gospel is thoroughly and mightily set forth by St. Paul in 2 Corinthians 3:7–9.

For this reason and in order that both doctrines, law and Gospel, may not be mingled together and confused so that what belongs to one doctrine is ascribed to the other, it is necessary to urge and to maintain with all diligence the true and proper distinction between law and Gospel, and diligently to avoid anything that might give occasion for a confusion between them by which the two doctrines would be tangled together made into one doctrine. (Article 5, sections 17, 20–22, 24–27)

1. How would you explain the difference between Law and Gospel to an inquirer?

2. C. F. W. Walther said, "Even if you were to quit your habitual cursing, swearing, and the like, that would not make you Christians" (*The Proper Distinction Between Law and Gospel*, CPH, p. 81). Explain how this statement is true.

3. "Put your confidence solely on the Lord Jesus Christ." In

what ways does your faith anchor your daily life?

VISION

Personal Reflection

1. During the past 24 hours, in what ways has God's Law revealed your sin? How has the Gospel comforted you?
2. In Thesis 62 of his Ninety-Five Theses, Luther said, "The true treasure of the church is the most holy gospel of the glory and grace of God." Explain.
3. What would eventually happen to you if you believed you could meet the demands of the Law? What would happen to you if you felt God wasn't serious about the Law or if you were ignorant of it?

Family Connection

1. Watch a television evangelist. Listen for clear teaching about God's Law and His Gospel. Analyze the spiritual value of the program based on the presentation of Law and Gospel.
2. Look at the Sunday school or vacation Bible school materials your children bring home. Ask them to find the words or pictures that show their need for Jesus. Also, ask them to find words or pictures that show Jesus as their Friend and Savior.
3. Make a habit of ending all family disputes and disciplinary situations with the same Gospel God left for all sinners. Think about it now. Plan your grace and Gospel words in the name of Jesus.

Closing Worship

Sing or pray together "The Savior Calls; Let Every Ear" (*LW* 350).

The Savior calls; let ev'ry ear
Attend the heav'nly sound.
O doubting souls, dismiss your fear;
Hope smiles reviving round.

For ev'ry thirsty, longing heart
Here streams of bounty flow
And life and health and bliss impart
To banish mortal woe

Here springs of sacred pleasures rise
To ease your ev'ry pain,
Immortal fountain, full supplies;
Nor shall you thirst in vain.

O sinners, come, hear mercy's voice;
The gracious call obey;
Mercy invites to heav'nly joys,
And can you yet delay?

For Next Week

Read Article 6 of the Formula of Concord (Epitome).

7

Article 6

FOCUS

Theme: The Third Function of the Law

Law/Gospel Focus

The Law condemns as it reveals our sin. It has no power to save. But the Law is a gift of God's goodness. He leaves us with no uncertainties about what He expects, and obedience to His Law would bring us nothing but happiness. In His love, God knew we could not obey Him, so He sent Jesus whose perfect obedience and sacrifice on the cross are our righteousness and salvation. In Christ alone we find our strength to love and follow God's Word.

Objectives

By the power of the Holy Spirit working through God's Word, we will

1. understand the role of the Law in the life of God's people;
2. identify differences between works of the Law and the fruit of the Spirit;
3. acknowledge the role of the effect of the Gospel on good works.

Opening Worship

Read together these words from 2 Corinthians 4 as a responsive prayer.

Leader: For we do not preach ourselves, but Jesus Christ as Lord, and ourselves as your servants for Jesus' sake.

Participants: For God, who said, "Let light shine out of darkness," made His light shine in our hearts to give us the light of the knowledge of the glory of God in the face of Christ.

Leader: But we have this treasure in jars of clay to show that this all-surpassing power is from God and not from us.

Participants: We are hard pressed on every side, but not crushed; perplexed, but not in despair;

Leader: Persecuted, but not abandoned; struck down, but not destroyed.

Participants: We always carry around in our body the death of Jesus, so that the life of Jesus may also be revealed in our body.

Leader: For we who are alive are always being given over to death for Jesus' sake,

Participant: so that His life may be revealed in our mortal body.

Introduction

In a continuing controversy about the legitimate place of God's Law in the life of the church, some early Lutherans, such as Agricola, continued to urge that the Law belonged neither in the church nor in the life of the regenerated child of God.

While it is true that Luther taught that the Law had no place in our lives *as far as justification is concerned,* he also taught that the Law condemns our sin and guides our understanding of what is God-pleasing. Article 6 of the Formula focuses on the Law and its functions.

1. What functions does Law have in secular society?

2. Which do you suppose people need to hear first: the Law or the Gospel? Why?

INFORM

The Formula of Concord: Epitome

The law has been given to men for three reasons: (1) to maintain external discipline against unruly and disobedient men, (2) to lead men to a knowledge of their sin, (3) after they are reborn, and although the flesh still inheres in them, to give them on that account a definite rule according to which they should pattern and regulate their entire life. It is concerning the third function of the law that a controversy has arisen among a few theologians. The question therefore is whether or not the law is to be urged upon reborn Christians. One party said Yes, the other says No.

1. We believe, teach, and confess that although people who genuinely believe and whom God has truly converted are freed through Christ from the curse and coercion of the law, they are not on that account without the law; on the contrary, they have been redeemed by the Son of God precisely that they should exercise themselves day and night in the law (Psalm 119:1). In the same way our first parents even before the Fall did not live without the law, for the law of God was written into their hearts when they were created in the image of God [Genesis 2:16; 3:3].

2. We believe, teach, and confess that the preaching of the law is to be diligently applied not only to unbelievers and the impenitent but also to people who are genuinely believing, truly converted, regenerated, and justified through faith.

3. For although they are indeed reborn and have been renewed in the spirit of their mind, such regeneration and renewal is incomplete in this world. In fact, it has only begun, and in the spirit of their mind the believers are in a constant war against their flesh (that is, their corrupt nature and kind), which clings to them until death [Galatians 5:17; Romans 7:21, 23]. On account of this Old Adam, who inheres in people's intellect, will, and all their powers, it is necessary for the law of God

constantly to light their way lest in their merely human devotion they undertake self-decreed and self-chosen acts of serving God. This is further necessary lest the Old Adam go his own self-willed way [Romans 12:7, 8]. He must be coerced against his own will not only by the admonitions and threats of the law, but also by its punishments and plagues, to follow the Spirit and surrender himself a captive. 1 Corinthians 9:27; Romans 6:12; Galatians 6:14; Psalm 119:1; Hebrews 13:21.

4. Concerning the distinction between works of the law and fruits of the Spirit we believe, teach, and confess that works done according to the law are, and are called, works of the law as long as they are extorted from people only under the coercion of punishments and the threat of God's wrath.

5. Fruits of the Spirit, however, are those works which the Spirit of God, who dwells in the believers, works through the regenerated, and which the regenerated perform in so far as they are reborn and do them as spontaneously as if they knew of no command, threat, or reward. In this sense the children of God live in the law and walk according to the law of God. In his epistles St. Paul calls it the law of Christ and the law of the mind. Thus God's children are "not under the law, but under grace" (Romans 7:23; 8:1, 14).

6. Therefore both for the penitent and impenitent, for regenerated and unregenerated people the law is and remains one and the same law, namely, the unchangeable will of God. The difference, as far as obedience is concerned, rests exclusively with man, for the unregenerated man—just like the regenerated according to the flesh—does what is demanded of him by the law under coercion and unwillingly. But the believer without any coercion and with a willing spirit, in so far as he is reborn, does what no threat of the law could ever have wrung from him.

Discussing the Text

1. What, in your own words, are the three functions of God's Law?

2. How do the confessors affirm the ongoing validity of the Law among God's redeemed people?

3. Why do "genuinely believing, truly converted" people need to hear the Law?

4. Describe the struggle believers have with their sinful nature.

5. What distinction do the confessors make between works of the Law and the fruit of the Spirit?

6. Create scenarios that characterize works of the Law and the fruit of the Spirit.

7. Why can the Law, in itself, never produce true righteousness?

CONNECT

At first glance, the difference between works of the Law and the fruit of the Spirit appears to be abstract, unrelated to our ordinary life. Yet knowing the difference brings joy to Christians because we see God's grace working through us as we serve Him and others. Good works done from a willing spirit are evidence of a lively, healthy faith, freed from slavery to the Law by Jesus Christ.

The Formula of Concord: Solid Declaration

> In order as far as possible to avoid all misunderstandings, to teach and to maintain the strict distinction between the works of the law and those of the spirit, we must observe with special diligence that in speaking of good works that are in accord with the law of God—for otherwise they are not good works—the

word "law" here has but one meaning, namely, the immutable [unchangeable] will of God according to which man is to conduct himself in this life. The distinction between works is due to the difference in the individuals who are concerned about living according to the law and the will of God. For as long as a person is not reborn, lives according to the law, and does its works merely because they are commanded, from fear of punishment or in hope of reward, he is still under the law. St. Paul calls the works of such a man "works of the law" [Romans 2:15; 3:20; Galatians 2:16; 3:2, 10] in the strict sense, because his good works are extorted by the law, just as in the case of bondservants. Such people are saints after the order of Cain.

But when a person is born anew by the Spirit of God and is liberated from the law (that is, when he is free from this driver and is driven by the Spirit of Christ), he lives according to the immutable will of God as it is comprehended in the law and, in so far as he is born anew, he does everything from a free and merry spirit. These works are, strictly speaking, not works of the law but works and fruits of the Spirit, or, as St. Paul calls them, the law of the mind and the law of Christ. According to St. Paul, such people are no longer under law but under grace (Romans 6:14; 8:2). Since, however, believers are not fully renewed in this life but the old Adam clings to them down to the grave, the conflict between spirit and flesh continues in them. According to the inmost self they delight in the law of God; but the law in their members is at war against the law of their mind. Thus though they are never without law, they are not under but in the law, they live and walk in the law of the Lord, and yet do nothing by the compulsion of the law. As far as the Old Adam who still adheres to them is concerned, he must be coerced not only with the law but also with miseries, for he does everything against his will and by coercion, just as the unconverted are driven and coerced into obedience by the threats of the law (1 Corinthians 9:27; Romans 7:18, 19).

Believers, furthermore, require the teaching of the law in connection with their good works, because otherwise they can easily imagine that their works and life are perfectly pure and holy. But the law of God prescribes good works for faith in such a way that, as in a mirror, it shows and indicates to them that in this life our good works are imperfect and impure. ...

The law demands a perfect and pure obedience if it is to please God. It does not teach us how and why the good works of believers are pleasing to God, even though in this life they are still imperfect and impure because of the sin in our flesh. But the Gospel teaches us that our spiritual sacrifices are acceptable to God through faith for Christ's sake (1 Peter 2:5; Hebrews 11:4; 13:15). In this respect Christians are not under the law but under grace because their persons have been freed from the curse and condemnation of the law through faith in Christ. Though their good works are still imperfect and impure, they are acceptable to God through Christ because according to their inmost self they do what is pleasing to God not by coercion of the law but willingly and spontaneously from the heart by the renewal of the Holy Spirit. (Article 6, sections 15–19, 21, 22–23)

1. In regard to good works, describe what is meant by the phrase "extorted by the law."

2. How does being "born anew by the Spirit" change the Christian's practice of good works?

3. In the light of Romans 12:1–2, share the joy and gratitude you have in offering yourself as a living sacrifice.

VISION

Personal Reflection

1. What were some of the good works you did last week? Which were routine and which were new? What prompted you to do those good things?
2. Was it difficult to recall your good works of the previous week? Why or why not? In what ways is that good or bad?
3. How might the devil lead you into spiritual danger through your good works?

Family Connection

1. Plant some marigold or bean seeds, and discuss what you can expect to grow. Let the grown plants remind you that from the seeds of faith grow the fruit of the Spirit.
2. Among the fruit of the Spirit are love, joy, and self-control. List some situations that you encounter every day; invite family members to say how they can express the fruit of the Spirit in words and actions.
3. Write the fruit of the Spirit from Galatians 5:22–23 on index cards. Once each week, have each family choose a card and recall how other family members or Christian acquaintances demonstrated that fruit. Then identify how you demonstrated it, thanking God for making you a fruitful person.

Closing Worship

Sing or pray together "How Precious Is the Book Divine" (*LW* 332).

How precious is the book divine,
By inspiration giv'n!
Bright as a lamp its teachings shine
To guide our souls to heav'n

Its light, descending from above,
Our gloomy world to cheer,
Displays our Savior's boundless love
And brings His glories near.

It shows to us our wand'ring ways
And where our feet have trod
And brings to view the matchless grace
Of our forgiving God.

This lamp through all the tedious night
Of life shall guide our way
Till we behold the clearer light
Of an eternal day.

For Next Week

Read Article 7 of the Formula of Concord (Epitome).

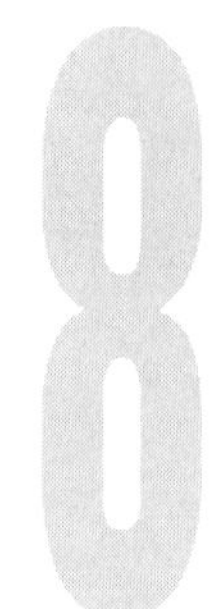

Article 7

FOCUS

Theme: The Holy Supper of Christ

Law/Gospel Focus

In His Holy Supper Jesus gives His body and blood in, with, and under bread and wine. Because of sin, we doubt His Word or distort His promise to be truly present in the Sacrament. The Holy Spirit works faith in our hearts to believe Christ's Word and to be faithful in receiving forgiveness, life, and salvation in the Lord's Supper.

Objectives

By the power of the Holy Spirit working through God's Word, we will

1. acknowledge and take to heart Christ's promise to be present in His Holy Supper;
2. repent of our failures to believe His Word and regularly partake of His body and blood;
3. rejoice in the great gift of Jesus, our Lord, in His Supper.

Opening Worship

Read together these words from 1 Corinthians 10 and 11 as a responsive prayer.

Leader: Is not the cup of thanksgiving for which we give thanks a participation in the blood of Christ?

Participants: And is not the bread that we break a participation in the body of Christ?

Leader: Because there is one loaf, we, who are many, are one body, for we all partake of the one loaf.

Participants: So whether you eat or drink or whatever you do, do it all for the glory of God.

Leader: For I received from the Lord what I also passed on to you: The Lord Jesus, on the night He was betrayed, took bread.

Participants: And when He had given thanks, He broke it and said, "This is My body, which is for you; do this in remembrance of Me."

Leader: In the same way, after supper He took the cup, saying, "This cup is the new covenant in My blood; do this, whenever you drink it, in remembrance of Me."

Participants: For whenever you eat this bread and drink this cup, you proclaim the Lord's death until He comes.

Introduction

By the late 1520s, sufficient discord on the true teaching concerning Holy Communion was present among the Reformers to cause them to meet at Marburg to hammer out their differences.

Ulrich Zwingli, the Swiss reformer, argued at the Marburg Colloquy that since flesh and spirit are incompatible, the presence of Christ in the Sacrament of Holy Communion can only be spiritual. To Zwingli it was "obvious" that the bread and wine of the Eucharist represent the *absent* body and blood of Christ.

Luther, however, drew a chalk circle on the meeting table and wrote, "This is My body." Luther's point was, of course, that the body and blood of Christ are truly present in the

Sacrament. For Luther the real presence was no harder to accept than the incarnation.

After Luther's death in 1546 it became increasingly clear that the same doctrinal division existed within the Lutheran camp. Lutherans held two positions—the "spiritualized" or "Sacramentarian" view (Christ is not physically present, but is received only by faith) and the view of the real presence. Article 7 defined the Lutheran and scriptural doctrine.

1. What different understandings of the Lord's Supper exist today?

2. Share a memory of your first communion.

INFORM

The Formula of Concord: Epitome

The question is, In the Holy Communion are the true body and blood of our Lord Jesus Christ truly and essentially present if they are distributed with the bread and the wine and if they are received orally by all those who use the sacrament, be they worthy or unworthy, godly or godless, believers or unbelievers, the believers for life and salvation, the unbelievers for judgment? ...

1. We believe, teach, and confess that in the Holy Supper the body and blood of Christ are truly and essentially present and are truly distributed and received with the bread and wine.

2. We believe, teach, and confess that the words of the testament of Christ are to be understood in no other way than in their literal sense, and not as though the bread symbolized the absent body and the wine the absent blood of Christ, but that because of the sacramental union they are truly the body and blood of Christ.

3. Concerning the consecration we believe, teach, and confess that no man's work nor the recitation of the minister effect

this presence of the body and blood of Christ in the Holy Supper, but it is to be ascribed solely and alone to the almighty power of our Lord Jesus Christ.

4. But at the same time we believe, teach, and confess with one accord that in the celebration of the Holy Supper the words of Christ's institution should under no circumstances be omitted, but should be spoken publicly, as it is written, "the cup of blessing which we bless" (1 Corinthians 10:16; 11:23–25). This blessing occurs through the recitation of the words of Christ.

5. The grounds on which we stand in this controversy with the Sacramentarians are those which Dr. Luther proposed in his *Great Confession*.

"The first ground is this article of our Christian faith: Jesus Christ is true, essential, natural, complete God and man in one person, inseparable and undivided.

"The second ground is: God's right hand is everywhere. Christ, really and truly set at this right hand of God according to His human nature, rules presently and has in His hands and under His feet everything in heaven and on earth. No other human being, no angel, but only Mary's Son, is so set down at the right hand of God, whence He is able to do these things.

"The third ground is that God's Word is not false nor does it lie.

"The fourth ground is that God has and knows various modes of being at a given place, and not only the single mode which the philosophers call *local* or spatial."

6. We believe, teach, and confess that with the bread and wine the body and blood of Christ are received not only spiritually, by faith, but also orally—however, not in a Capernaitic manner, but because of the sacramental union in a supernatural and heavenly manner. The words of Christ teach this clearly when they direct us to take, eat, and drink, all of which took place in the case of the apostles, since it is written, "And they all drank of it" (Mark 14:23). Likewise, St. Paul says, "The bread which we break, is it not a participation in the body of Christ?" (1 Corinthians 10:16)—that is, whoever eats this bread eats the body of Christ. ...

7. We believe, teach, and confess that not only the genuine believers and those who are worthy but also the unworthy and the unbelievers receive the true body and blood of Christ; but if they are not converted and do not repent, they receive them not to life and salvation but to their judgment and condemnation.

For although they reject Christ as a redeemer, they must accept Him even contrary to their will as a strict judge. He is just as much present to exercise and manifest His judgment on unrepentant guests as He is to work life and consolation in the hearts of believing and worthy guests.

8. We believe, teach, and confess that there is only one kind of unworthy guest, namely, those who do not believe. Of such it is written, "He who does not believe is condemned already" (John 3:18). The unworthy use of the holy sacrament increases, magnifies, and aggravates this condemnation (1 Corinthians 11:27, 29).

9. We believe, teach, and confess that no genuine believer, no matter how weak he may be, as long as he retains a living faith, will receive the Holy Supper to his condemnation, for Christ instituted this Supper particularly for Christians who are weak in faith but repentant, to comfort them and to strengthen their weak faith.

10. We believe, teach, and confess that the entire worthiness of the guests at this heavenly feast is and consists solely and alone in the most holy obedience and complete merit of Christ, which we make our own through genuine faith and of which we are assured through the sacrament. Worthiness consists not at all in our own virtues or in our internal and external preparations.

Discussing the Text

1. Describe the real presence of Christ in His Holy Supper.

2. Why, according to the confessors, is a symbolic view of the Lord's Supper inadequate?

3. How does Article 7 affirm the consecration in the Lord's Supper?

4. What are the four grounds for the real presence as Luther writes in his *Great Confession*?

5. The word *Capernaitic* refers to the wrong understanding of the people of Capernaum (John 6:26–52). What was their understanding of the words of Jesus?

6. Who receives the body and blood of Christ in His Holy Supper? What important distinction do the confessors make between recipients?

7. Who is a worthy guest at the Lord's Table?

8. How does the Lord's Supper comfort and strengthen believers?

CONNECT

Some people avoid Holy Communion because they think they are too sinful to participate in such a holy act. Yet the first recipients of the Lord's Supper were certainly sinners, and they would soon abandon the Lord in fear and faithlessness. Jesus' gift was graciously simple: His body and blood for our life! His supper is for us! By the grace of God, we, too, receive forgiveness and power through the Sacrament.

The Formula of Concord: Solid Declaration

It is our Lord and Savior Jesus Christ concerning whom, as our unique teacher, the earnest command has been given from heaven to all men, "Listen to Him." He is not a mere man or an angel; He is not only truthful, wise, and mighty, but Himself the eternal truth and wisdom and the almighty God. He knows very well what and how He must speak, and He is able mightily to accomplish and achieve what He speaks and promises, as He says, "Heaven and earth shall pass away, but My words will not pass away" [Luke 21:33], and again, "All authority in heaven and on earth has been given to Me" [Matthew 28:18]. After the Last Supper, as He was about to begin His bitter passion and death for our sin, in this sad, last hour of His life, this truthful and almighty Lord, our Creator and Redeemer Jesus Christ, selected His words with great deliberation and care in ordaining and instituting this most venerable sacrament, which was to be observed with great reverence and obedience until the end of the world and which was to be an abiding memorial of His bitter passion and death and of all His blessings, a seal of the new covenant, a comfort for all sorrowing hearts, and a true bond and union of Christians with Christ their head and with one another. Under these circumstances Christ said of the blessed and proffered bread, "Take, eat, this is My body which is given for you" [Matthew 26:26; Luke 22:19], and concerning the cup or the wine, "This is My blood of the new covenant which is shed for you for the remission of sins" [Mark 14:24; Luke 22:20; Matthew 26:28].

We are therefore bound to interpret and explain these words of the eternal, truthful, and almighty Son of God, Jesus Christ, our Lord, Creator, and Redeemer, not as flowery, figurative, or metaphorical expressions, as they appear to our reason, but we must accept them in simple faith and due obedience in their strict and clear sense, just as they read. Nor dare we permit any objection or human contradiction, spun out of human reason, to turn us away from these words, no matter how appealing our reason may find it. Abraham certainly had sufficient ground for a disputation when he heard God's words about offering up his son, because these words were patently contrary not only to reason and to divine and natural law but also to the eminent article of faith concerning the promised seed, Christ, who was to be born of Isaac. He could have asked if this command was to be understood literally or if it was to receive a tolerable and loose interpretation. But as on the previous occasion when Abraham received the promise of the blessed seed of Isaac, although this seemed impossible to his reason, he gave God the honor of truthfulness and concluded and believed most certainly in his heart that what God promised He was also able to do. So Abraham understood and believed the words and command of God plainly and simply, as the words read, and committed the entire matter to God's omnipotence and wisdom, knowing that God had many more ways and means of fulfilling the promises concerning the seed of Isaac than he could comprehend with his blind reason. In the same way we are to believe in all humility and obedience the explicit, certain, clear, and earnest words and commands of our Creator and Redeemer, without any doubts or arguments as to how it is to be reconciled with our reason or how it is possible. The Lord who has spoken these words is Himself infinite Wisdom and Truth and can certainly accomplish and bring to pass whatever He promises. (Article 7, sections 43–47)

1. Describe Abraham's trust in God's promises. How is faith in Christ's promises similar?

2. In what ways do the confessors rely on Christ's word and His promises to fulfill His Word?

3. How has the Lord's Supper brought you comfort in life?

VISION

Personal Reflection

1. What would you say to someone who asked you to explain how bread and wine can be Christ's body and blood?
2. Is there anything you may want to begin or stop doing in your preparation to receive Holy Communion?
3. Why should you participate in the Lord's Supper even when you feel the burden of your sins? What should you do when your sins don't feel like a burden?

Family Connection

1. Ask family members to relate their favorite miracle

recorded in the Bible. Remind each other of the miracle that still occurs every time the Lord's Supper is served.

2. Ask your pastor if you or younger family members can accompany him on a Communion visit to shut-ins. Prepare for some simple conversation that adds a fellowship dimension to otherwise private Communion.

Closing Worship

Sing or pray together "O Lord, We Praise You" (*LW* 238).

O Lord, we praise You, bless You, and adore You,
In thanksgiving bow before You.
Here with Your body and Your blood You nourish
Our weak souls that they may flourish.
O Lord, have mercy!
May Your body, Lord, born of Mary,
That our sins and sorrows did carry,
And Your blood for us plead
In all trial, fear, and need:
O Lord, have mercy!

Your holy body into death was given,
Life to win for us in heaven.
No greater love than this to You could bind us;
May this feast of that remind us!
O Lord, have mercy!
Lord, Your kindness so much did move You
That Your blood now moves us to love You.
All our debt You have paid;
Peace with God once more is made.
O Lord, have mercy!

May God bestow on us His grace and favor
To please Him with our behavior
And live together here in love and union
Nor repent this blest communion.
O Lord, have mercy!
Let not Your good Spirit forsake us,
But that heav'nly minded He make us;
Give Your church, Lord, to see

Days of peace and unity.
O Lord, have mercy!

For Next Week

Read Article 8 of the Formula of Concord (Epitome).

Article 8

FOCUS

Theme: The Person of Christ

Law/Gospel Focus

Jesus Christ is both true God and true man—one person. In the incarnation, the Son of God came down from heaven and was born of the Virgin Mary for us and for our salvation. Although human beings may reject His coming or doubt His promises, Jesus is the Lord whose death and resurrection bring salvation to all who believe. Through Baptism, we are God's beloved children in Christ.

Objectives

By the power of the Holy Spirit working through God's Word, we will

1. recognize Jesus as the God-man, who is fully divine and fully human;
2. identify the attributes that describe Jesus' divine and human natures;
3. appreciate the reasons why Jesus was both God and man.

Opening Worship

Read together these words from 1 Corinthians 15 as a responsive prayer.

Leader: For what I received I passed on to you as of first importance: that Christ died for our sins according to the Scriptures,

Participants: That He was buried, that He was raised on the third day according to the Scriptures, and that He appeared to Peter, and then to the Twelve.

Leader: But if it is preached that Christ has been raised from the dead, how can some of you say that there is no resurrection of the dead?

Participants: If there is no resurrection of the dead, then not even Christ has been raised.

Leader: And if Christ has not been raised, our preaching is useless and so is your faith.

Participants: Then those also who have fallen asleep in Christ are lost.

Leader: But Christ has indeed been raised from the dead, the firstfruits of those who have fallen asleep.

Participants: For since death came through a man, the resurrection of the dead comes also through a man.

Leader: For as in Adam all die, so in Christ all will be made alive.

Participants: But each in His own turn: Christ, the firstfruits; then, when He comes, those who belong to Him.

Introduction

Jesus Christ, the God-man. On the basis of Scripture the Lutheran church refused to accept the notion that in Christ there was merely a fusing of the two natures or that either nature was changed by virtue of the incarnation.

Rather, with Luther, the confessors affirmed that in Christ there is one person with two natures. Jesus Christ is truly man and truly God; He is both fully human and fully divine, the one Savior. This position is set forth in Article 8.

1. What do people say about Jesus, God's Son?

2. What do people say about Jesus, the man?

INFORM

The Formula of Concord: Epitome

The chief question has been, Because of personal union in the person of Christ, do the divine and human natures, together with their properties, *really* (that is, in deed and truth) share with each other, and how far does this sharing extend? ...

To explain and to settle this controversy according to our Christian faith we teach, believe, and confess the following:

1. That the divine and the human natures are personally united in Christ in such a way that there are not two Christs, one the Son of God and the other the Son of man, but a single individual is both the Son of God and the Son of man (Luke 1:35; Romans 9:5).

2. We believe, teach, and confess that the divine and the human nature are not fused into one essence and that the one is not changed into the other, but that each retains its essential properties and that they never become the properties of the other nature.

3. The properties of the divine nature are omnipotence, eternity, infinity, and (according to its natural property, by itself) omnipresence, omniscience, etc., which never become properties of the human nature.

4. The attributes of the human nature are to be a corporeal creature, to be flesh and blood, to be finite and circumscribed, to suffer, to die, to ascend and to descend, to move from place to place, to endure hunger, thirst, cold, heat, and the like, which never become the properties of the divine nature.

5. Since both natures are united personally (that is, in one person) we believe, teach, and confess that this personal union is not a combination or connection of such a kind that neither nature has anything in common with the other personally (that

is, on account of the personal union), as when two boards are glued together and neither gives anything to or takes anything from the other. On the contrary, here is the highest communion which God truly has with man. Out of this personal union and the resultant exalted and ineffable sharing there flows everything human that is said or believed about God and everything divine that is said or believed about Christ the man. The ancient Fathers have illustrated this union and sharing of the natures by the analogy of incandescent iron and the union of body and soul in man.

6. Therefore we believe, teach, and confess that God is man and man is God, which could not be the case if the divine and human natures did not have a real and true communion with each other.

For how could the man, Mary's son, truly be called or be God, or the Son of the most high God, if His humanity were not personally and truly united with the Son of God and hence really (that is, in deed and in truth) shared only the name of God with the divine nature?

7. Therefore we believe, teach, and confess that Mary conceived and bore not only a plain, ordinary, mere man but the veritable Son of God; for this reason she is rightly called, and truly is, the mother of God.

8. Therefore we also believe, teach, and confess that it was not a plain, ordinary, mere man who for us suffered, died, was buried, descended into hell, rose from the dead, ascended into heaven, and was exalted to the majesty and omnipotent power of God, but a man whose human nature has such a profound and ineffable union and communion with the Son of God that it has become one person with Him.

9. Therefore the Son of God has truly suffered for us, but according to the property of the human nature which He assumed into the unity of His divine person and made His own, so that He could suffer and be our high priest for our reconciliation with God, as it is written in 1 Corinthians 2:8, They have "crucified the Lord of glory," and in Acts 20:28, We are purchased with God's own blood.

10. Therefore we believe, teach, and confess that the Son of man according to His human nature is really (that is, in deed and in truth) exalted to the right hand of the omnipotent majesty and power of God, because He was assumed into God when He was conceived by the Holy Spirit in His mother's

womb and His human nature was personally united with the Son of the Most High.

11. According to the personal union He always possessed this majesty. But in the state of His humiliation He dispensed with it and could therefore truly increase in age, wisdom, and favor with God and men, for He did not always disclose this majesty, but only when it pleased Him. Finally, after His resurrection He laid aside completely the form of a slave [Philippians 2:7] (not the human nature) and was established in the full use, revelation, and manifestation of His divine majesty. Thus He entered into His glory in such a way that now not only as God, but also as man, He knows all things, can do all things, is present to all creatures, and has all things in heaven and on earth and under the earth beneath His feet and in His hands [John 13:3], as He Himself testifies, "All authority in heaven and on earth has been given to Me" [Matthew 28:18], and as St. Paul states, He ascended "far above all the heavens that He might fill all things" [Ephesians 4:10]. He exercises His power everywhere omnipresently, He can do everything, and He knows everything.

Discussing the Text

1. How would you describe Christ to an inquirer?

2. What are the properties of the divine nature of Christ? How did Christ display His divine nature in His ministry?

3. What are the properties of the human nature of Christ? How did He display His human nature?

4. Why do the confessors keep the two natures distinct but united in one person?

5. Describe, as possible, the personal union. How do the analogies of incandescent iron (glowing) and body and soul in human beings help to explain this unique union?

6. Why can believers truly confess, "Our God died!"?

7. Describe the state of humiliation.

8. Describe the state of exaltation.

CONNECT

Have any gods of any civilization ever presented themselves as a sacrifice? The one, true God loved His people so much that He became flesh in Jesus in order to suffer and die in payment for *our* sins. We wonder, How can Jesus be both true God and true man? While certain parallels help us understand, we live by faith, not by sight. God has told us the truth about Himself in the Word; by His grace, we believe.

The Formula of Concord: Solid Declaration

> Because of this personal union and the resultant communion that the divine and human natures have with each other in deed and truth in the person of Christ, things are attributed to Christ according to the flesh that the flesh, according to its nature and essence outside of this union, cannot intrinsically be or have ... [O]nly this man and no other human being in heaven and on earth can say truthfully, "Where two or three are gathered in My name, there am I in the midst of them" [Matthew 18:20], likewise, "I am with you always even to the close of the age" [Matthew 18:20]. We do not understand these testimonies to mean that only the deity of Christ is present with

us in the Christian church and community and that this presence of Christ in no way involves His humanity. If that were true, Peter, Paul, and all the saints in heaven would also be with us on earth because the Godhead which is everywhere dwells in them. The Scriptures ascribe such presence only to Christ, and to no other human being. We believe that the cited passages illustrate the majesty of the man Christ, which Christ received according to His humanity at the right hand of the majesty and power of God, so that, also according to and with this same assumed human nature of His, Christ can be and is present wherever He wills, and in particular that He is present with His church and community on earth as mediator, head, king, and high priest. Not part or only one-half of the person of Christ, but the entire person to which both natures, the divine and the human, belong is present. He is present not only according to His deity, but also according to and with His assumed human nature, according to which He is our brother and we flesh of His flesh and bone of His bone (Ephesians 5:30). To make certainty and assurance doubly sure on this point, He instituted His Holy Supper that He might be present with us, dwell in us, work and be mighty in us according to that nature, too, according to which He has flesh and blood.

On the basis of this solid foundation, Dr. Luther, of blessed memory, has written about the majesty of Christ according to the human nature. In the *Great Confession concerning the Holy Supper* he writes about the person of Christ: "Since He is a man like this—and apart from this man there is no God—it must follow that ... He is and can be everywhere that God is and that everything is full of Christ through and through, also according to the humanity—not, of course, according to the first, corporeal, comprehensible manner, but according to the supernatural, divine manner. Here you must take your stand and say that wherever Christ is according to the deity, He is there as a natural, divine person and is also naturally and personally there, as His conception in His mother's womb proves conclusively. For if He was the Son of God, He had to be in His mother's womb naturally and personally and become man. But if He is present naturally and personally wherever He is, then He must be man there, too, since He is not two separate persons but a single person. Wherever this person is, it is the single, indivisible person, and if you can say, 'Here is God,' then you must also say, 'Christ the man is

> present too.'... Wherever you put God down for me, you must also put the humanity down for me. They simply will not let themselves be separated and divided from each other. He has become one person and never separates the assumed humanity from Himself. (Article 8, sections 76–84)

1. In what ways is Christ's deity important in your life? His humanity?

2. Christ is and can be everywhere that God is. Describe the comfort God's people have in this simple truth.

3. Read Hebrews 4:14–16. Which phrases refer to Christ as God? As man? How are both Good News for sinners?

VISION

Personal Reflection

1. Read Luther's explanation to the Second Article of the Apostles' Creed.
2. One phrase of the explanation stands out: "That I may be His own." Aside from the peace offered by this phrase, what are its implications for the believer?
3. How can you express your gratitude for the "for you" nature of the incarnation ("who for us men and for our salvation came down from heaven")?

Family Connection

1. Purchase an artist's rendering of Jesus and display it in your home. As an alternative, ask a young child to draw a picture of Jesus for his or her bedroom.
2. Place an empty chair in a room where you pray or con-

duct devotions. Let it illustrate Matthew 18:20: "For where two or three come together in My name, there am I with them."

3. Have children draw pictures of both the Christmas and Easter stories. Then ask them to narrate the story of Jesus' birth and His death and resurrection.

Closing Worship

Sing or pray together "O Savior, Precious Savior" (*LW 282*).

O Savior, precious Savior, Whom yet unseen we love;
O name of might and favor, All other names above;
We worship You; we bless You; To You alone we sing;
We praise You and confess You, Our holy Lord and King.

O Bringer of salvation, So marvelously wrought,
Yourself the revelation Of love beyond our thought:
We worship You; we bless You; To You alone we sing;
We praise You and confess You, Our holy Lord and King.

In You all fullness dwelling, All grace and pow'r divine;
Your glory all excelling, God's Son, O Savior mine.
We worship You; we bless You; To You alone we sing;
We praise You and confess You, Our holy Lord and King.

For Next Week

Read Article 9 of the Formula of Concord (Epitome).

Article 9

FOCUS

Theme: Christ's Descent into Hell

Law/Gospel Focus

God's people take comfort in Christ's victory preached to the spirits in prison (1 Peter 3:19). By our sin we are deserving of eternal death and hell, but by God's grace we have been rescued from sin, death, and the devil through the saving work of Jesus.

Objectives

By the power of the Holy Spirit working through God's Word, we will

1. understand that Jesus descended into hell to proclaim His victory over all enemies;
2. rejoice in the comfort His triumph brings to our lives;
3. demonstrate a desire to share His saving Gospel with others;

Opening Worship

Read together these words from 1 Corinthians 15 as a responsive prayer.

Leader: I declare to you, brothers, that flesh and blood cannot inherit the kingdom of God, nor does the perishable inherit the imperishable.

Participants: Listen, I tell you a mystery: We will not all sleep, but we will all be changed—

Leader: In a flash, in the twinkling of an eye, at the last trumpet. For the trumpet will sound, the dead will be raised imperishable, and we will be changed.

Participants: For the perishable must clothe itself with the imperishable, and the mortal with immortality.

Leader: When the perishable has been clothed with the imperishable, and the mortal with immortality, then the saying that is written will come true: "Death has been swallowed up in victory."

Participants: "Where, O death, is your victory? Where, O death, is your sting?"

Leader: The sting of death is sin, and the power of sin is the law.

Participants: But thanks be to God! He gives us the victory through our Lord Jesus Christ.

Introduction

The controversy over Christ's descent into hell was at first limited to the German city of Hamburg. Lutheran Pastor John Aepinus wondered if the descent was part of Christ's humiliation or exaltation and if it occurred before or after Christ's resurrection.

Other pastors in Hamburg suggested that Christ's words on the cross, "It is finished" (John 19:30), made it clear that His suffering (and the state of humiliation) was ended at His death. Hamburg's city council, in order to bring theological peace to their community, solicited an opinion from Philip Melanchthon.

Melanchthon's indecisive answer actually caused the controversy to spread beyond Hamburg. The authors of the Formula of Concord settled the issue by referring to a sermon preached by Martin Luther in Torgau in 1533. Luther counseled simple acceptance of Christ's descent into hell as a confession on Christ's victory.

1. What types of victory today do people announce?

2. Describe a time when you wanted to share good news with others.

INFORM

The Formula of Concord: Epitome

There has been a dispute among some theologians of the Augsburg Confession concerning this article also. The questions raised were: When and how, according to our simple Christian Creed, did Christ go to hell? Did it happen before or after His death? Did it occur only according to the soul, or only according to the deity, or according to body and soul, spiritually or corporeally? Does this article belong to Christ's suffering or to His glorious victory and triumph?

This article, like the preceding one, cannot be comprehended with our senses and reason, but must be apprehended by faith alone. Therefore it is our unanimous opinion that we should not engage in disputations concerning this article, but believe and teach it in all simplicity, as Dr. Luther of blessed memory taught in his sermon preached at Torgau in the year 1533, where he explains this article in a wholly Christian manner, eliminates all unnecessary questions, and admonishes all Christians to simplicity of faith.

It is enough to know that Christ went to hell, destroyed hell for all believers, and has redeemed them from the power of death, of the devil, and of the eternal damnation of the hellish jaws. How this took place is something that we should postpone until the other world, where there will be revealed to us not only this point, but many others as well, which our blind reason cannot comprehend in this life but which we simply accept.

Discussing the Text

1. In what ways did Christ confront sin, death, Satan, and hell in His ministry?

2. "It is finished" (John 19:30). Explain the Lord's words from the cross.

3. Why do the confessors insist that the descent into hell must be understood by faith alone?

4. How does Luther describe Christ's victory in his *Personal Prayer Book* (1522)?

> I believe that for me and all His believers Christ descended into hell to subdue the devil (1 Peter 3:18–20) and take him captive alone with all his power, cunning, and malice so that the devil can no longer harm me, and that He redeemed me from the [eternal] pains of hell, transforming them into something nondestructive and beneficial [for the believer].

5. In what ways is reason an obstacle in understanding Christ's descent into hell?

6. Describe how the descent to hell is a "Gospel celebration."

CONNECT

I believe! God's people could not say these words at all were it not for the Holy Spirit who brings us to faith and keeps us in faith. Believing is more powerful than understanding because God's mysterious power extends beyond intellect. By faith we trust what the Bible reports is true: Jesus conquered sin and death and gives us His victory through our Baptism into His death and resurrection.

The Formula of Concord: Solid Declaration

> Different explanations of the article on Christ's descent into hell have been discovered among some of our theologians just as among the ancient teachers of the Christian church. Hence we let matters rest on the simple statement of our Christian Creed, to which Dr. Luther directs us in the sermon that he

held in the castle at Torgau in the year 1533, "I believe in the Lord Christ, God's Son, who died, was buried, and descended into hell." Herein the burial and the descent into hell are differentiated as distinct articles, and we simply believe that after the burial the entire person, God and man, descended into hell, conquered the devil, destroyed hell's power, and took from the devil all his might.

We are not to concern ourselves with exalted and acute speculations about how this occurred. With our reason and five senses this article cannot be comprehended any more than the preceding one, how Christ has been made to sit at the right hand of the almighty power and majesty of God. We must only believe and cling to the Word. Then we shall retain the heart of this article and derive from it the comfort that neither hell nor the devil can take us or any believer in Christ captive or harm us. (Article 9, sections 1–3)

1. In what ways is Christ's descent and victory a proclamation of comfort to the dying? To those plagued by guilt?

2. What does it mean to "cling to the Word" in your life?

3. Share the joy you have in your *eternal* victory through Christ.

VISION

Personal Reflection

1. Watch a news program and note sin's effect on life. Imagine, if you can, how Christ's power over sin will be demonstrated in heaven for eternity.
2. Read the obituaries in several issues of a newspaper. Look for statements of faith that express the comfort of everlasting life.

3. How is your life different, knowing that Christ has defeated sin and Satan?

Family Connection

1. Share how your family can face death and dying with confidence through Christ.
2. Compose a family prayer, thanking God for defeating sin and for His promise to take His people to live in heaven with Jesus.
3. Plan and design your Easter decorations for the next festival of the resurrection.

Closing Worship

Sing or pray together "The Day of Resurrection" (*LW* 133).

The day of resurrection! Earth, tell it out abroad,
The passover of gladness, The passover of God.
From death to life eternal, From sin's dominion free,
Our Christ has brought us over With hymns of victory.

Now let the heav'ns be joyful, Let earth its song begin,
Let all the world keep triumph And all that is therein.
Let all things, seen and unseen, Their notes of gladness blend;
For Christ the Lord has risen, Our joy that has no end!

Then praise we God the Father, And praise we Christ His Son,
With them the Holy Spirit, Eternal Three in One,
Till all the ransomed number Fall down before the throne
And honor, pow'r, and glory Ascribe to God alone!

For Next Week

Read Article 10 of the Formula of Concord (Epitome).

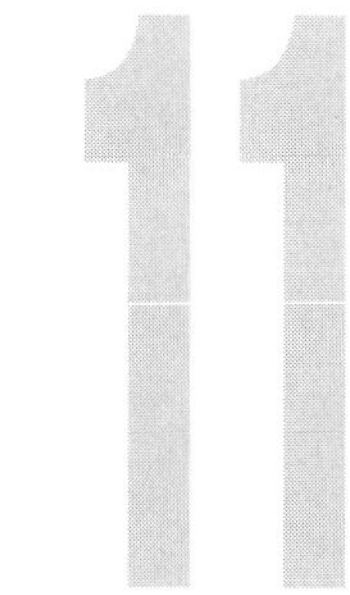

Article 10

FOCUS

Theme: Church Usages

Law/Gospel Focus

The Gospel of forgiveness, life, and salvation brings genuine freedom. In Christ, God's people are rescued from slavery to sin, death, and Satan. The Holy Spirit works faith in our hearts through Word and Sacrament and strengthens us to worship and to serve in love.

Objectives

By the power of the Holy Spirit working through God's Word, we will

1. understand that Christ has won freedom for us through His death and resurrection;
2. rejoice that the Holy Spirit works in our lives;
3. live in our Gospel freedom as we make God-pleasing decisions by the Spirit's guidance and power.

Opening Worship

Read together these words from 2 Corinthians 5 as a responsive prayer.

Leader: For Christ's love compels us, because we are convinced that one died for all, and therefore all died.

Participants: And He died for all, that those who live should no longer live for themselves but for Him who died for them and was raised again.

Leader: So from now on we regard no one from a worldly point of view. Though we once regarded Christ in this way, we do so no longer.

Participants: Therefore, if anyone is in Christ, he is a new creation; the old has gone, the new has come!

Leader: All this is from God, who reconciled us to Himself through Christ and gave us the ministry of reconciliation:

Participants: That God was reconciling the world to Himself in Christ, not counting men's sins against them. And He has committed to us the message of reconciliation.

Leader: We are therefore Christ's ambassadors, as though God were making His appeal through us. We implore you on Christ's behalf: Be reconciled to God.

Participants: God made Him who had no sin to be sin for us, so that in Him we might become the righteousness of God.

Introduction

After Luther's death, the Holy Roman Empire demanded that Lutherans observe certain church rites as divinely instituted because they were mandated by the pope. Melanchthon played a leading role in a "compromise," which was soon rejected by some of his contemporaries.

The Lutherans of southern Germany especially resisted both the Augsburg and Leipzig Interims (Agreements) of 1548. These Lutheran pastors and people, urged on by Flacius, declared themselves to be *in a state of confession*. Compromise under persecution and demand, they said, was a compromise of the Gospel itself.

In 1556 Melanchthon admitted that he had made a mistake. But the controversy rolled onward. It took the firmness and clarity of Article 10 to settle the issue for the divided Lutherans.

1. In what ways is it difficult to "stand up for" what you believe?

2. When might compromise be acceptable in the church?

INFORM

The Formula of Concord: Epitome

The chief question has been, In times of persecution, when a confession is called for, and when the enemies of the Gospel have not come to an agreement with us in doctrine, may we with an inviolate conscience yield to their pressure and demands, reintroduce some ceremonies that have fallen into disuse and that in themselves are indifferent things and are neither commanded nor forbidden by God, and thus come to an understanding with them in such ceremonies and indifferent things? One party said Yes to this, the other party said No.

1. To settle this controversy we believe, teach, and confess unanimously that the ceremonies or church usages which are neither commanded nor forbidden in the Word of God, but which have been introduced solely for the sake of good order and the general welfare, are in and for themselves no divine worship or even a part of it. "In vain do they worship Me, teaching as doctrines the precepts of men" (Matthew 15:9).

2. We believe, teach, and confess that the community of God in every locality and every age has authority to change such ceremonies according to circumstances, as it may be most profitable and edifying to the community of God.

3. But in this matter all frivolity and offenses are to be avoided, and particularly the weak in faith are to be spared (1 Corinthians 8:9–13; Romans 14:13ff).

4. We believe, teach, and confess that in time of persecution,

when a clear-cut confession of faith is demanded of us, we dare not yield to the enemies in such indifferent things, as the apostle Paul writes, "For freedom Christ has set us free; stand fast therefore, and do not submit again to a yoke of slavery" (Galatians 5:1). "Do not be mismated with unbelievers, for what fellowship has light with darkness?" (2 Corinthians 6:14). "To them we did not yield submission even for a moment, that the truth of the Gospel might be preserved for you" (Galatians 2:5). In such a case it is no longer a question of indifferent things, but a matter which has to do with the truth of the Gospel, Christian liberty, and the sanctioning of public idolatry, as well as preventing offense to the weak in faith. In all these things we have no concessions to make, but we should witness an unequivocal confession and suffer in consequence what God sends us and what He lets the enemies inflict on us.

5. We believe, teach, and confess that no church should condemn another because it has fewer or more external ceremonies not commanded by God, as long as there is mutual agreement in doctrine and in all its articles as well as in the right use of the holy sacraments. ...

Discussing the Text

1. What tension did the confessors face in this issue?

2. Explain the term "indifferent things." Give examples.

3. Describe the authority God's people have to change church usages. Why might the church make these changes?

4. In what ways can indifferent things contribute to good order and general welfare in the church?

5. In what ways can indifferent things threaten freedom in Christ and His Gospel?

6. On what points were the confessors *unwilling* to compromise?

7. Describe how believers may be sensitive to fellow believers who are weak in faith.

8. In what ways does Article 10 uphold and affirm genuine freedom in Christ?

CONNECT

The life, death, and resurrection of the Lord Jesus has set us free to live in the grace of God. Within that freedom is the privilege to worship using a variety of expressions, so long as they are in agreement with God's Word. Whatever rituals, ceremonies, or order of services we choose, we take care not to dilute the Gospel or pervert God's truth. By God's grace, His people aspire to worship and serve Christ the Savior in confident faith and bold freedom.

The Formula of Concord: Solid Declaration

> For here we are no longer dealing with the external adiaphora which in their nature and essence are and remain of themselves free and which accordingly are not subject either to a command or a prohibition, requiring us to use them or to discontinue them. Here we are dealing primarily with the chief article of our Christian faith, so that, as the apostle testifies, the truth of the Gospel might be preserved (Galatians 2:5). Any coercion or commandment darkens and perverts this article because the adversaries will forthwith publicly demand such matters of indifference to confirm false doctrines, superstition, and idolatry and to suppress the pure doctrine and Christian liberty, or they will misuse them and misinterpret them in this direction.

At the same time this concerns the article of Christian liberty as well, an article which the Holy Spirit through the mouth of the holy apostle so seriously commanded the church to preserve, as we have just heard. As soon as this article is weakened and human commandments are forcibly imposed on the church as necessary and as though their omission were wrong and sinful, the door has been opened to idolatry, and ultimately the commandments of men will be increased and be put as divine worship not only on a par with God's commandments, but even above them.

Hence yielding or conforming in external things, where Christian agreement in doctrine has not previously been achieved, will support the idolaters in their idolatry, and on the other hand, it will sadden and scandalize true believers and weaken them in their faith. As he values his soul's welfare and salvation, every Christian is obligated to avoid both, as it is written, "Woe to the world for temptations to sin" [Matthew 18:7], and again, "Whoever causes one of these little ones who believe in me to sin, it were better for him to have a great millstone fastened around his neck and to be drowned in the depth of the sea" [Mattehw 18:6]. We are to be particularly mindful that Christ says, "So everyone who acknowledges Me before men, I also will acknowledge before My Father who is in heaven" (Matthew 10:32). (Article 10, sections 14–17)

1. In what ways has freedom in Christ been a blessing in your life?

2. How is idolatry a danger when external forms of worship or rituals become mandatory?

3. Which practices of your congregation do you most enjoy? Why?

4. Which practices of your congregation would you like to change? Why?

VISION

Personal Reflection

1. Create a brief and simple order of service for daily, personal devotions. Evaluate what you could change in your service and what should remain constant.
2. Watch a variety of religious services on television. Which ones focus on Jesus as our Savior? On what do others focus?
3. Write a letter to your pastor or congregation stating your gratitude for leadership in worship practices. Cite those attributes that you most appreciate.

Family Connection

1. Discuss the parts of your congregational worship that you do not understand. Share ways that you can grow in appreciation for worship.
2. Visit another church of your denomination. Discuss similarities and differences between the congregation you visit and your home congregation.
3. Use a variety of worship resources for family devotions—songbooks, devotional readings, prayer books, and the like. Ask your pastor to recommend books consistent with Scripture and the Confessions.

Closing Worship

Sing or pray together "Christ Is Our Cornerstone" (*LW* 290).

Christ is our cornerstone,
On Him alone we build;
With His true saints alone
The courts of heav'n are filled.
On His great love
Our hopes we place
Of present grace
And joys above.

Oh, then, with hymns of praise
These hallowed courts shall ring;
Our voices we will raise
The Three in One to sing
And thus proclaim
In joyful song,
Both loud and long,
That glorious name.

Here, gracious God, do now
And evermore draw near;
Accept each faithful vow,
And ev'ry suppliant hear.
In copious show'r
On all who pray
Each holy day
Your blessing pour.

Here may we gain from heav'n
The grace which we implore,
And may that grace, once giv'n,
Be with us evermore
Until that day
When all the blest
To endless rest
Are called away.

For Next Week

Read Article 11 of the Formula of Concord (Epitome).

Article 11

FOCUS

Theme: God's Eternal Foreknowledge and Election

Law/Gospel Focus

Through God's free grace and favor and by the power of the Spirit, we receive God's gift of eternal salvation. No human being earns a place among the elect, although in our sinful lack of faith we may seek to be justified by what we do. God's mercy in Christ anchors our faith and enables us to praise God for His sure promise.

Objectives

By the power of the Holy Spirit working through God's Word, we will

1. understand the truth of God's Word about God's foreknowledge and election in Christ;
2. rejoice that through faith we give all glory and honor to God alone for our salvation;
3. seek the comfort that election in Christ provides for our hearts, assailed each day as we are by sin, death, and the devil.

Opening Worship

Read together these words from 2 Corinthians 5 as a responsive prayer.

Leader: Now we know that if the earthly tent we live in is destroyed, we have a building from God, an eternal house in heaven, not built by human hands.

Participants: Meanwhile we groan, longing to be clothed with our heavenly dwelling,

Leader: Because when we are clothed, we will not be found naked.

Participants: For while we are in this tent, we groan and are burdened, because we do not wish to be unclothed but to be clothed with our heavenly dwelling, so that what is mortal may be swallowed up by life.

Leader: Now it is God who has made us for this very purpose and has given us the Spirit as a deposit, guaranteeing what is to come.

Participants: Therefore we are always confident and know that as long as we are at home in the body we are away from the Lord.

Leader: We live by faith, not by sight.

Participants: So we make it our goal to please Him whether we are at home in the body or away from it.

Introduction

Lutherans of the 16th-century were never in public disagreement on the doctrine of God's foreknowledge and election. The confessors included an article on this subject to provide comfort for God's faithful people and to lay a doctrinal foundation for future generations.

The Lutherans were united in their stance against the Calvinistic approach to the doctrine of salvation, namely, that God has arbitrarily decided both that some will be saved and others will be condemned. Upholding God's desire for the salvation of all and the sufficiency of Christ's redemptive work, Article 11 confesses the scriptural truth of election.

1. Why do you think there was little controversy among Lutherans regarding election?

2. What misunderstanding do people have about election?

INFORM

The Formula of Concord: Epitome

No public dissension has developed among the theologians of the Augsburg Confession concerning this article. But since it is such a comforting article when it is correctly treated, we have included an explanation of it in this document, lest at some future date offensive dissension concerning it might be introduced into the church.

1. To start with, the distinction between the foreknowledge and the eternal election of God is to be diligently noted.

2. God's foreknowledge is nothing else than that God knows all things before they happen, as it is written, "There is a God in heaven who reveals mysteries, and He has made known to King Nebuchadnezzar what will be in the latter days" (Daniel 2:28).

3. This foreknowledge extends alike over good people and evil people. But it is not a cause of evil or of sin which compels anyone to do something wrong; the original source of this is the devil and man's wicked and perverse will. Neither is it the cause of man's perdition; for this man himself is responsible. God's foreknowledge merely controls the evil and imposes a limit on its duration, so that in spite of its intrinsic wickedness it must minister to the salvation of His elect.

4. Predestination or the eternal election of God, however, is concerned only with the pious children of God in whom He is well pleased. It is a cause of their salvation, for He alone brings it about and ordains everything that belongs to it. Our salvation is so firmly established upon it that the "gates of Hades cannot prevail against it" (John 10:28; Matthew 16:18).

5. We are not to investigate this predestination in the secret counsel of God, but it is to be looked for in His Word, where He has revealed it.

6. The Word of God, however, leads us to Christ, who is "the book of life" [Philippians 4:3; Revelation 3:5; 20:15] in which all who are to be eternally saved are inscribed and elected, as it is written, "He chose us in Him before the foundation of the world" (Ephesians 1:4).

7. This Christ calls all sinners to Himself and promises them refreshment. He earnestly desires that all men should come to Him and let themselves be helped [Matthew 9:2, 9, 13, 22, 29, 35, 37; 11:28]. To these He offers Himself in His Word, and it is His will that they hear the Word and do not stop their ears or despise it. In addition He promises the power and operation of the Holy Spirit and divine assistance for steadfastness and eternal life.

8. Therefore we should not judge this election of ours to eternal life on the basis either of reason or of God's law. This would either lead us into a reckless, dissolute, Epicurean life, or drive men to despair and waken dangerous thoughts in their hearts. As long as men follow their reason, they can hardly escape such reflections as this: "If God has elected me to salvation I cannot be damned, do as I will." Or, "If I am not elected to eternal life, whatever good I do is of no avail; everything is in vain in that case."

9. We must learn about Christ from the holy Gospel alone, which clearly testifies that "God has consigned all men to disobedience, that He may have mercy upon all" (Romans 11:32), and that He does not want anyone to perish (Ezekiel 33:11; 18:23), but that everyone should repent and believe on the Lord Jesus Christ (1 Timothy 2:6; 1 John 2:2).

Discussing the Text

1. What is the distinction between God's foreknowledge and His eternal election?

2. Explain why God's foreknowledge is not the cause of events or human actions.

3. Describe how predestination or eternal election is rooted exclusively in God's grace revealed in Christ.

4. What promises does Christ give to His elect?

5. "If God has elected me to salvation, I cannot be damned, do as I will." Why is this way of thinking wrong?

6. "If I am not elected to eternal life, whatever good I do is of no avail; everything is in vain in that case." Why is this way of thinking wrong?

7. How would you explain God's saving will in Christ to a nonbeliever?

CONNECT

The faith God's people confess in the Apostles' Creed is *saving* faith. It is a gift of God bestowed by the Holy Spirit through Word and Sacrament. In Christ, we take comfort and praise God that He has chosen us to be His redeemed children. We do not concern ourselves with the complexities that sometimes arise in the study of election or predestination. An inquisitive and rational mind will urge us to "make sense" of election. Through Christ, however, we rest content in His promise: life and salvation!

The Formula of Concord: Solid Declaration

> This teaching and explanation of the eternal and saving election of the elect children of God gives God His due honor fully

and completely. It sets forth that He saves us "according to the purpose" of His will through sheer mercy in Christ without our merit and good works, as it is written, "He destined us in love to be His son through Jesus Christ, according to the purpose of His will, and to the praise of His glorious grace which He freely bestowed on us in the Beloved" (Ephesians 1:5, 6). It is therefore false and wrong when men teach that the cause of our election is not only the mercy of God and the most holy merit of Christ, but that there is also within us a cause of God's election on account of which God has elected us unto eternal life. For not only before we had done any good, but even before we were born [Romans 9:11] (in fact, "Before the foundation of the world was laid" [Ephesians 1:4]) God elected us in Christ—"in order that God's purpose of election might continue, not because of works but because of His call, she was told, 'The elder will serve the younger.' As it is written, "Jacob I loved, but Esau I hated' " (Romans 9:11–13; Genesis 25:23; Malachi 1:2, 3).

Moreover, when people are taught to seek their eternal election in Christ and in His holy Gospel as the "book of life," this doctrine never occasions either despondency or a riotous and dissolute life. This does not exclude any repentant sinner but invites and calls all poor, burdened, and heavy-laden sinners to repentance, to a knowledge of their sins, and to faith in Christ and promises them the Holy Spirit to cleanse and renew them. This doctrine gives sorrowing and tempted people the permanently abiding comfort of knowing that salvation does not rest in their own hands. If this were the case, they would lose it more readily than Adam and Eve did in paradise—yes, would be losing it every moment and hour. Their salvation rests in the gracious election of God, which He has revealed to us in Christ, out of whose hand "no one can pluck" us (John 10:28; 2 Timothy 2:19). Hence if anyone so sets forth this teaching concerning God's gracious election that sorrowing Christians can find no comfort in it but are driven to despair, or when impenitent sinners are strengthened in their malice, then it is clearly evident that this teaching is not being set forth according to the Word and will of God but according to reason and the suggestion of the wicked devil. For the apostle testifies that "Whatever was written in former days was written for our instruction, that by steadfastness and by encouragement of the Scriptures we might have hope" (Romans 15:4). But it is certain that any interpretation of the Scriptures which weakens or even removes this comfort and hope is contrary to the Holy Spirit's will and intent. We shall abide by this simple, direct, and useful exposition which is permanently and well grounded in God's revealed will, we shall avoid and flee all abstruse and specious questions and disputations, and we reject and condemn all those things which are contrary to these true, simple, and useful expositions. (Article 11, sections 87–93)

1. In what ways does the truth about election give "God His due honor fully and completely"?

2. Describe how election is a comforting, encouraging doctrine.

3. What are the dangers of going beyond God's Word to explain election?

4. How will you express your gratitude to God for His election in Christ?

VISION

Personal Reflection

1. What tools has the Holy Spirit provided to help you grow as a result of your election? How will you use them?
2. Consider how God's election differs from earthly elections. For what will you praise God?

Family Connection

1. We like being chosen for good things! Think about God choosing you as His child (John 15:16). Make a family mural of praise.

2. Walk through a cemetery, commenting on the variety of names and ages of those buried there. Discuss why cemeteries are sometimes sad places. Also, discuss why they are also happy places.
3. Ask why questions to which no adequate answer exists. For example, Why did God put so many stars in the sky? Conclude the questions-without-answers session by agreeing that God alone knows these answers. Only God knows all things. Thank God for His unfathomable knowledge!

Closing Worship

Sing or pray together "Love in Christ Is Strong and Living" (*LW* 376).

Love in Christ is strong and living,
Binding faithful hearts in one;
Love in Christ is true and giving.
May His will in us be done.

Love is patient and forbearing,
Clothed in Christ's humility,
Gentle, selfless, kind and caring,
Reaching out in charity.

Love in Christ abides forever,
Fainting not when ills attend;
Love, forgiving and forgiven,
Shall endure until life's end.

For Next Week

Read Article 12 of the Formula of Concord (Epitome).

Article 12

FOCUS

Theme: Other Churches

Law/Gospel Focus

Left to our own strength and resources, God's people cannot continue in faith and the confession of His saving truth. Yet God in His mercy forgives our sin and failures. By the Spirit, we are united with Christ in Baptism and therefore grow in faith, hope, and love, nourished and strengthened through Word and Sacrament.

Objectives

By the power of the Holy Spirit working through God's Word, we will

1. recognize the doctrinal errors identified by the authors and signers of the Formula of Concord;
2. recognize and formulate responses to additional errors we can identify today;
3. praise God for doctrine fully founded upon Scripture.

Opening Worship

Read together these words from 2 Corinthians 9 as a responsive prayer.

Leader: Remember this: Whoever sows sparingly will also reap sparingly, and whoever sows generously will also reap generously.

Participants: Each man should give what he has decided in his heart to give, not reluctantly or under compulsion, for God loves a cheerful giver.

Leader: And God is able to make all grace abound to you, so that in all things at all times, having all that you need, you will abound in every good work.

Participants: As it is written: "He has scattered abroad His gifts to the poor: His righteousness endures forever."

Leader: Now He who supplies seed to the sower and bread for food will also supply and increase your store of seed and will enlarge the harvest of your righteousness.

Participants: You will be made rich in every way so that you can be generous on every occasion, and through us your generosity will result in thanksgiving to God.

Introduction

As the confessors concluded their statement of faith. They included a final article on the false teachings of other churches and sects. The Anabaptists—the word means "to rebaptize"—were scattered across Europe, but they shared the conviction that Baptism was for the regenerated only. They rejected infant Baptism, denied original sin, and denied that Baptism and Holy Communion were means of grace which give the forgiveness of sins. The Schwenkfelders were followers of Caspar Schwenkfeld, who rejected the full deity of Christ and the ministry of Word and Sacrament. The New Arians were unitarians: they rejected the doctrine of the Trinity and acknowledged Christ as subordinate to the Father. The Anti-Trinitarians also denied the triune God and believed in three separate divine beings.

Article 12 of the Formula addresses these serious errors in the church and world.

1. How, from your perspective, do doctrinal errors in the church arise?

2. In what ways is the church today struggling against false teaching?

INFORM

The Formula of Concord: Epitome

In the preceding explanation we have made no mention of the errors held by these factions. But lest as a result of our silence these errors be attributed to us, we wish here at the end merely to enumerate the articles in which they err and contradict our repeatedly cited Christian Creed and Confession.

Errors of the Anabaptists

1. That Christ did not assume His body and blood from the virgin Mary, but brought them with Him from heaven.

2. That Christ is not true God but that He only has more gifts of the Holy Spirit than any other holy person.

3. That our righteousness before God does not consist wholly in the unique merit of Christ, but in renewal and in our own pious behavior. For the most part this piety is built on one's own individual self-chosen spirituality, which in fact is nothing else but a new kind of monkery.

4. That in the sight of God unbaptized children are not sinners but are righteous and innocent, and that as long as they have not achieved the use of reason they will be saved in this innocence without Baptism (which according to this view they do not need). They thus reject the entire doctrine of original sin and everything that pertains to it.

5. That children are not to be baptized until they have achieved the use of reason and can confess their faith personally.

6. That without and prior to Baptism the children of Chris-

tian parents are holy and the children of God by virtue of their birth from Christian and pious parents. ...

7. That a congregation is not truly Christian if sinners are still found in it.

8. That no one should hear sermons or attend services in those temples where formerly ... Masses were read and celebrated.

9. That one is to have nothing to do with clergymen who preach the Gospel according to the Augsburg Confession and reprove the preaching and the errors of the Anabaptists; nor should one serve them or work for them in any way, but flee and avoid them as perverters of God's Word.

Errors of the Schwenkfelders

1. That all who say that Christ according to the flesh is a creature do not have a right understanding of Christ as the reigning king of heaven.

2. That in Christ's glorification His flesh received all the divine properties in such a way that Christ as man is fully equal in rank and essential estates to the Father and to the Word as far as might, power, majesty, and glory are concerned, and that now both natures in Christ possess only one divine essence, property, will, and glory and that the flesh of Christ belongs to the essence of the holy Trinity.

3. That the ministry of the church—the Word preached and heard—is not a means through which God the Holy Spirit teaches people and creates in them the saving knowledge of Christ, conversion, repentance, faith, and new obedience.

4. That the water of Baptism is not a means through which the Lord God seals the adoption of children and effects rebirth.

5. That bread and wine in the Holy Supper are not means through and by which Christ distributes His body and blood.

6. That a Christian who is truly born again through the Spirit of God can perfectly keep and fulfill the law of God in this life.

7. That it is no true Christian congregation in which public expulsion and the orderly process of excommunication do not take place.

8. That a minister of the church cannot teach profitably or administer true and genuine sacraments unless he is himself truly reborn, righteous, and pious.

Error of the New Arians

That Christ is not a true, essential, natural God, of one divine essence with God the Father and the Holy Spirit, but is merely adorned with divine majesty and is inferior to and beside God the Father.

Error of the Anti-Trinitarians

This is an entirely new sect, unknown in Christendom until now, which believes, teaches, and confesses that there is not only one eternal, divine essence, belonging to the Father, Son, and Holy Spirit, but as God the Father, Son and Holy Spirit are three distinct persons, so each person has its distinct divine essence, separate from the other persons of Deity. Some maintain that each of the three has the same power, wisdom, majesty, and glory, just like any three individual people who are essentially separate from one another. Others maintain that the three are unequal in essence and properties and that only the Father is rightly and truly God.

Discussing the Text

1. In what ways do the errors listed in Article 12 undermine the Gospel?

2. Why, do you suppose, is original sin and infant Baptism a "stumbling block" in our day, too?

3. "If a congregation still has sinners, it's not truly Christian." True or false? Explain your answer.

4. How did some reject the means of grace in the confessors' day? What remains without the Word and the sacraments?

5. "Christ is inferior to God the Father." Respond.

6. "The Father, the Son, and the Holy Spirit. See, we worship three Gods." Respond.

7. Why was it important for the confessors to include Article 12?

CONNECT

God has richly blessed His people with His holy Word—the Bible. He has also blessed us with confessions of faith, public statements that present His truth in concise, simple language. Through these Confessions, He has kept generations of believers faithful to His Word, and He has protected them from doctrines that would mislead Christians or undermine their faith.

The Formula of Concord: Solid Declaration

> All these and similar articles, and whatever attaches to them or follows from them, we reject and condemn as false, erroneous, heretical, contrary to the Word of God, to the three Creeds, to the Augsburg Confession and the Apology, to the Smalcald Articles, to Luther's Catechisms. All pious Christians will and should avoid these as dearly as they love their soul's welfare and salvation.
>
> Therefore, in the presence of God and of all Christendom among both our contemporaries and our posterity, we wish to have testified that the present explanation of all the foregoing controverted articles here explained, and none other, is our teaching, belief, and confession in which by God's grace we shall appear with intrepid hearts before the judgment seat of Jesus Christ and for which we shall give an account. Nor shall we speak or write anything, privately or publicly, contrary to this confession, but we intend through God's grace to abide by it. (Article 12, sections 39–40)

1. Why is it important for God's people to avoid false teaching?

2. How does regular continued Bible study help Christians hold fast to God's truth in the Gospel?

3. How can you grow in your understanding of and appreciation for *your* Confessions?

VISION

Personal Reflection

1. Obtain a copy of Luther's Small Catechism, and regularly review the summaries of Christian doctrine.
2. Obtain information about other denominations to determine how their doctrines differ from the Confessions. (Many denominations host an Internet site.)
3. Having completed this study, you have a good background in sound, Christian doctrine. Consider teaching Sunday school, a youth Bible class, or a small group.

Family Connection

1. As you pray with family members, thank God for bringing you to faith, solely by His love.
2. Next time you witness infant Baptism, discuss why it's appropriate to baptize babies. Praise God for sending the Holy Spirit to young children.
3. Fold several sheets of paper in half, and make a homemade book telling and illustrating how each family member came to faith.

Closing Worship

Sing or pray together "Jesus, Still Lead On" (*LW* 386).

Jesus, still lead on
Till our rest be won;
And although the way be cheerless,
We will follow calm and fearless;
Guide us by Your hand
To our fatherland.

If the way be drear,
If the foe be near,
Let no faithless fears o'er take us;
Let not faith and hope forsake us;
Safely past the foe
To our home we go.

Jesus, still lead on
Till our rest be won;
Heav'nly leader, still direct us,
Still support, console, protect us,
Till we safely stand
In our fatherland.